I dedicate this book to planet Earth. May we aim to nurture and repair it through our choices and actions.

Contents

INTRODUCTION

Hello everyone, and welcome to my third book! While I know cookbooks are supposed to be a learning tool for those reading them, I, too, have learned so much from writing these. When I did *Vegan Bowl Attack!* I felt that I needed to "go big or go home," which I most certainly did! Then, I opted for simpler recipes in *Vegan Yack Attack on the Go!* to make it a beginner-friendly book for those of you with less time in your schedules. Now, I'm here with *Vegan Yack Attack's Plant-Based Meal Prep*, where I've taken both of those concepts and melded them in a dynamic, delicious way. The result is a book that will help you get organized and make your life easier.

Because I've been a recipe developer and food photographer since 2011, I've never prioritized meal prep. I would pretty much eat whatever I was working on at the time, which was kind of convenient—except for weeks where desserts were the only thing on the menu. That may sound like a "princess problem," but it has been hard to find balance at times!

Just after starting this book, I became a total convert. Having delicious, well-rounded meals like smoothie jars and protein bowls ready in the fridge whenever hunger struck was amazing! It ensured that I wasn't shoving a handful of peanut butter pretzels in my mouth and calling it lunch. I had so much more energy throughout the day that even my partner, Corey, got on board.

Unlike my other titles, I've included approximate nutrition analysis for these recipes, which has also been enlightening. I am typically an intuitive eater, but it was affirming to see how rich in nutrition those recipes with a grain, protein, and veggies really were. Goes to show that it's not hard to get enough protein through vegan meals!

I wrote this book in order of cooking experience level. Part one is a general introduction to meal planning and prepping, with lots of tips on how to stock your kitchen. Part two is for all you beginners out there: five-day meal plans for just one person. Since each menu relies on just a few entrees, they're easy to prepare on a day off so they'll be ready for your work week! The menus are limited in quantity (but not flavor) so that newbies to meal prep and vegan food don't get too overwhelmed.

Part three is for those who are already established home cooks but are sick of repeating the same things over and over again. These meal plans for families, or just for two, break down, step by step, how to prep a week's worth of meals and meal components. Each menu is laid out in an easy-to-read table, so you can see just what to expect that week. All of the recipes are in the chapters in parts three and four.

It is also in those recipe chapters that more experienced cooks can let their creativity shine. Maybe once you've grown accustomed to my suggested menus, you want to branch out—absolutely do it! One week when you don't feel like meal prepping or planning, you can just thumb through the book and make whatever you want.

I hope that this cookbook will be as helpful for you as it was for me, and that it will show you, and those around you, how attainable—and tasty— eating a plant-based diet can be.

Even if planning doesn't come to you naturally, getting your hands on this book is a great start! I'll make the planning process as seamless as possible, with helpful organizing tips, advice on equipment and tools, and a breakdown of the recipe labels.

TIPS ON ORGANIZING

There are two reasons why it's called "meal planning" and not "leftover cooking." First, one sounds more appetizing than the other, and second, because planning out your meals makes your life easier for the rest of the week.

• When in doubt, make a list. Though I have sorted out shopping lists for the weekly meal plans for one—and have the recipes ordered in the most time-efficient way—lists can help you stay organized, even if you go rogue. Figure out all of the recipes you want to make for the week. When you're ready to begin preparing ingredients, do all of your mise en place, meaning chopping, measuring, and sorting, before any cooking starts. This is especially helpful if you have recipes that share ingredients, such as diced onions, spices, grains, and more. There's no sense in going back and forth to a commonly used ingredient! Next, take a look at which recipe parts may take the longest to cook, chill, roast, etc. Start your cooking process with those, then move on to quicker items that you can prepare while the first ones are cooking.

• If you start to feel overwhelmed, know that getting all of these meals and snacks done in the same couple of hours saves you so much time during the week. Soon, that weight will lift and turn into relief. Another way to share the load is to delegate certain duties to another person, say a significant other, roommate, or child. Most of the sauces in this book are either whisked in a bowl or made in a blender, which is a task even the most inexperienced home cooks can do. Plus, if you plan a meal-prep day each week, it turns into a "date" of sorts for spending time and learning together.

• Let me be the first one to say that, though I've done my best to make my weekly menus cater to all kinds of people, there is no one-size-fits-all approach with meal prepping. If you need to add or take items out to fit your nutritional needs, go ahead! Does one menu not have enough calories for your lifestyle? Add some more calorie-dense or protein-rich ingredients to the recipes, or prep more items from the snack chapter.

ESSENTIAL MEAL-PREP EQUIPMENT

I remember the first time my dude, Corey, wanted to meal prep for himself but knew nothing about cooking, so I was enlisted to help. Because he was starting from nothing, we needed to stock his kitchen. That experience taught me the basic building blocks of weekly meal planning that you can use to conquer your own prepping.

Storage containers: Sturdy, stackable containers will be one of your best friends throughout this process. It's worth it to invest in some resilient glass containers with snap-on lids. I find that these keep the most air out, and do not crack or oxidize like plastic containers. If you're dipping your toe into meal prepping and are not sure you want to spend the dough on glass containers, I suggest getting packs of dishwasher-safe takeout containers. They store easily, won't break the bank, and if you lose some or do not end up sticking with your plan, it's not the end of the world. Reusable glass jars also come in handy!

Pots and pans: Having an assortment of pots and pans is key to getting your home-cook on. These basics will cover a lot of what we will be doing in this book! Meal prepping means bulk cooking, so having at least one large pan and one large pot is very helpful. If you're a beginner, you may want to get nonstick pans and pots, such as those with ceramic coatings; the learning curve is not as steep, and sautéing requires less oil.

Utensils: Of course, utensils are a must! Typically, I use silicone spoons and spatulas because they are heat resistant and easy to clean; plus, they won't scratch up your nonstick cookware. You can also buy silicone-coated whisks. A ladle, a can opener, a citrus reamer or press, tongs, a peeler, and a grater are also all very helpful. Having a sharp knife is key for safe, efficient ingredient prep, and you really need only one.

Measuring cups and mixing bowls: How are you going to prep your ingredients and components without measuring and mixing? For this, have measuring spoons, dry measuring cups, wet measuring cups, and mixing bowls on hand. Having a small kitchen scale is immensely helpful for setting up your recipes and dividing portions for the week.

Baking sheets: For your roasting and baking needs, be sure to have two large baking sheets and parchment paper. If you see yourself roasting often, consider buying a silicone baking mat so that you don't go through as much parchment paper. I also suggest having one 12-count muffin or cupcake pan; it is great for making quiche bites, chocolate cups, protein muffins, and more! It also doesn't hurt to have one large casserole dish, especially for items like lasagna.

Blender and food processor: My blender is one of the most-used small appliances in my kitchen. You will usually find me using it a couple times a day, and it is so versatile. Smoothies, sauces, soups, fillings, and more can be made in a blender, which can also double as a food processor—though I prefer to have both. Refurbished high-speed blenders are fairly affordable and worth every penny, if you're in need of one.

Extras: There are also a few items that aren't 100 percent essential but are supremely helpful. An Instant Pot, pressure cooker, slow cooker, and/or air fryer all streamline the cooking process and make it easier in their own ways. If you invest in an Instant Pot, you get a pressure cooker, slow cooker, and several other functions all in one appliance. I love the Instant Pot for meal prepping because it can cook grains quickly and steam heaps of vegetables in 2 minutes. Wild, right? An air fryer is basically a compact convection oven, which means that a fan moves hot air around the food quickly so that the cooking time is shorter. Because of its small size, an air fryer is best for small-batch cooking or for reheating leftovers. If you have the space and budget, bringing these two countertop appliances into your kitchen will change your life.

HELPFUL INGREDIENTS TO STOCK

A vegan pantry is not all that different from its nonvegan counterpart, but there are changes in quantities and a few interesting items added to the mix. Here is a basic list of what you need on hand to make delicious and complete meals!

Fruits and vegetables: This should go without saying, but keeping your fridge and pantry stocked with your favorite fruits and veggies makes cooking at home infinitely easier. For further convenience, stock your freezer with some options so you don't have to worry about them going bad.

Herbs and spices: Having plenty of dried herbs and spices on your shelf makes it easy to customize recipe flavors in no time at all. A bonus seasoning that you definitely need is nutritional yeast; it is an inactive yeast rich in B vitamins and it adds a savory flavor to many vegan dishes. Keeping vegetable bouillon cubes or concentrate on hand means you don't have to store quarts and quarts of veggie broth.

Dried and canned beans: All colors and varieties of beans are great sources of protein and fiber, plus they're super versatile in recipes. An important note: I use a lot of canned beans in my recipes. If you prefer to cook your own, know that one 15-ounce (425 g) can of beans is usually 1½ cups (273 g) to 1⅝ cups (300 g) of cooked beans.

Grains of all kinds: Brown rice, jasmine rice, long-grain white rice, quinoa, millet, buckwheat, and farro are some of my favorites.

Tempeh, tofu, and seitan: These are three cornerstones of vegan protein. Tempeh and tofu are made with soybeans and can be gluten-free, while seitan is made from vital wheat gluten, a protein that comes from wheat. You can even make your own seitan (page 45). Tofu, tempeh, and seitan are all great for marinating or seasoning with any flavors you desire.

Nuts and seeds: Some of my most used nuts and seeds are cashews, almonds, walnuts, pumpkin seeds, sesame seeds, sunflower seeds, and chia seeds. I use them in many recipes in this book, and they are also great for making vegan versions of dairy and eggs.

Dry goods: Flours, starches, and pastas are used throughout my recipes. Because they are shelf-stable, they are good to have on hand at all times.

Liquids: I keep oils, vinegars, and nondairy milks stocked for a wide variety of meal-prep situations. I use organic sunflower oil for most of my high-temperature cooking, olive oil for dressings, and coconut oil for baking. Apple cider, rice, and balsamic vinegars are my most commonly used and are easily found at your local grocer. As for nondairy milks, I stick to plain, unsweetened kinds so that they can be used in both savory and sweet recipes.

Convenience items: It is pretty easy to come by vegan versions of cheeses, creams, meats, sauces, etc. While a lot of what is in this cookbook can be made at home, you can customize or save time using some of the store-bought substitutes.

RECIPE LABELS

For each recipe, you'll see labels that will let you know a little more about it. Some refer to the cooking process and the qualities of the dish, while others refer to allergy-friendliness and diet restrictions.

• FRESH OUTTA THE FRIDGE

These are dishes that can be made ahead of time and eaten cold after being stored.

• NEEDS SOME HEAT

These dishes can be prepped ahead of time, but should be reheated for best quality and flavor.

• FREEZER FRIENDLY

Not all food that goes into the freezer comes out okay on the other end, but these ones are perfect for freezing!

• 30 MINUTES OR LESS

The quickest and easiest recipes of the bunch.

• UNDER 10 INGREDIENTS

These recipes will use ten ingredients or fewer, not counting salt, pepper, or water.

• GLUTEN FREE

These recipes do not use ingredients that contain gluten. You will also see "Gluten-free option" for those recipes where an easy gluten-free swap can be made.

• SOY FREE

These recipes do not contain soy products. You'll see "Soy-free option" where you can make a soy-free swap, such as using coconut aminos instead of tamari.

• NUT FREE

These recipes do not contain nuts or nut products, such as nut butters or oils. I've also included "Nut-free option" where the nuts can be removed from the recipe or replaced with a no-nut option like sunflower seeds.

• OIL FREE

Recipes with this tag do not contain any oils.

• NO SUGAR ADDED

Outside of naturally occurring sugar in raw food ingredients, these recipes contain no extra sugar.

Part 2

WEEKLY MEAL PREP FOR ONE

HOW THE MENUS WORK

In this section, each menu contains three main entrees, which will provide five full days of meals, plus two snacks for the week. This type of prep is perfect for those who need some serious organizational assistance, as your entire work week is covered! Note that the shopping lists contain some items that will not be completely used up at the end of your prep—don't worry, these ingredients are used throughout the book, so they won't go to waste (try putting them to use in your weekend cooking). Once you've stocked your pantry for one menu, you won't have to purchase the entire shopping list for the next menu, since single containers of oils, spices, or nut butters will last for a while.

WEEKLY MENU 1

- **BEGINNER**
- **GLUTEN-FREE OPTION**

Breakfast: **Overnight Chai Chia Pudding** (page 18)
Lunch: **Curried Tofu Wraps** (page 19)
Dinner: **Chimichurri Chickpea Kale Bowl** (page 20)
Snacks: **Lemon Quinoa Bites** (page 144) and **Spicy Crusted Kelp Chips** (page 149)

SHOPPING LIST

Produce

- ☐ 2 pounds (907 g) pears
- ☐ 1 small head red cabbage
- ☐ 12 ounces (335 g) kale
- ☐ 16-ounce (455 g) package cremini or baby bella mushrooms
- ☐ 2 red or orange bell peppers
- ☐ 1 red onion
- ☐ 1 head garlic
- ☐ 1 bunch cilantro
- ☐ 1 bunch flat-leaf parsley
- ☐ 1 small package fresh oregano
- ☐ 3 limes
- ☐ 2 lemons

Grocery

- ☐ 2 (15-ounce [425 g]) cans chickpeas
- ☐ 1 (13.5-ounce [400 ml]) can full-fat coconut milk
- ☐ 1 package of burrito-sized tortillas, gluten-free if necessary
- ☐ 1 package of nori seaweed sheets
- ☐ 1 small package panko, gluten-free if necessary
- ☐ 1 small bag brown rice flour
- ☐ 1 small package dried dates
- ☐ 1 jar/container of tahini
- ☐ 1 bottle tamari or coconut aminos
- ☐ 1 small bottle sriracha or similar chile sauce
- ☐ 1 bottle olive oil
- ☐ 1 bottle sunflower oil
- ☐ 1 can cooking spray
- ☐ 1 bottle red wine vinegar
- ☐ 1 small bottle agave nectar
- ☐ 1 small bottle vanilla extract
- ☐ 1 small box chai tea bags

Refrigerator

- ☐ 2 (14-ounce [397 g]) packages firm tofu
- ☐ 1 quart (945 ml) unsweetened almond milk

Bulk

- ☐ 2 cups (346 g) quinoa
- ☐ 1 cup (163 g) chia seeds
- ☐ ½ cup (40 g) quick-cooking oats
- ☐ 1 cup (145 g) raw almonds
- ☐ ½ cup (55 g) chopped pecans

Dried Herbs and Spices

- ☐ Yellow curry powder
- ☐ Onion powder
- ☐ Ground ginger
- ☐ Crushed red pepper
- ☐ Salt
- ☐ Black pepper

GUIDELINES FOR PREPPING

Step 1: Prepare and bake the curried tofu. While the tofu is baking, combine the quinoa and water from both the Chimichurri Chickpea Kale Bowls and the Lemon Quinoa Bites and cook it on the stove.

Step 2: While the quinoa is cooking, make and store the Overnight Chai Chia Pudding and the Chimichurri. Once the tofu is done baking, make the Spicy Crusted Kelp Chips.

Step 3: While the chips are baking, finish assembling and storing the Curried Tofu Wraps. Divide the cooked quinoa in half and use half to make the Lemon Quinoa Bites.

Step 4: Assemble and store the Chimichurri Chickpea Kale Bowls. Allow the Spicy Crusted Kelp Chips to cool, then store.

OVERNIGHT CHAI CHIA PUDDING

• FRESH OUTTA THE FRIDGE • UNDER 10 INGREDIENTS
• GLUTEN FREE • SOY FREE • OIL FREE

I'm a huge fan of adding caffeinated beverages to my morning meals, and the comforting flavor of chai spice makes it perfect for this chia pudding! While the base is subtly flavored, the diced pears and pecans offer welcome sweetness and crunch.

2 cups (475 ml) boiling water
2 chai tea bags
2½ cups (570 ml) unsweetened almond milk
¼ cup (60 ml) agave nectar
1 teaspoon vanilla extract
Pinch salt
1 cup (163 g) chia seeds
2 pounds (907 g) pears, cored and diced
½ cup (55 g) chopped pecans

In a large liquid measuring cup or bowl, pour the boiling water over the tea bags and steep for 7 to 10 minutes, depending on how strong you prefer the tea flavor to be. Discard the tea bags, squeezing out as much liquid as possible, and whisk the almond milk, agave nectar, vanilla, and salt into the tea. Stir in the chia seeds and divide the loose mixture between 5 jars or airtight containers.

Divide the pears and pecans evenly among the jars. Cover the jars and refrigerate for at least 8 hours or up to 5 days.

YIELD: 5 SERVINGS

NUTRITIONAL ANALYSIS
Per serving: 417 calories; 19 g fat; 53 g carbohydrates; 22 g fiber; 27 g sugar; 12 g protein

CURRIED TOFU WRAPS

• FRESH OUTTA THE FRIDGE • GLUTEN-FREE OPTION
• NUT FREE • NO SUGAR ADDED

These Curried Tofu Wraps are like a tornado of flavors, colors, and textures! Firm, baked tofu combined with a creamy tahini sauce and crunchy veggies make these wraps simple, but oh so delicious.

FOR THE TOFU:

2 (14-ounce [397 g]) packages firm tofu, drained and rinsed

Cooking spray

1½ tablespoons (10 g) yellow curry powder

2 teaspoons (5 g) onion powder

½ teaspoon salt

½ teaspoon black pepper

FOR THE COCONUT-TAHINI SAUCE:

½ cup (120 ml) full-fat coconut milk, stirred well

⅓ cup (80 g) tahini

3 tablespoons (45 ml) lime juice

¼ teaspoon salt

FOR THE ASSEMBLY:

5 burrito-sized flour tortillas or 10 small gluten-free wraps

2½ cups (225 g) shredded red cabbage

2 red or orange bell peppers, stemmed, seeded, and sliced into strips

½ cup (840 g) thinly sliced red onion

¼ cup (4 g) loosely packed fresh cilantro

To make the tofu: Preheat the oven to 400°F (200°C, or gas mark 6) and line a baking sheet with parchment paper. Wrap the tofu in a kitchen towel or paper towels, place something heavy on top of it (books or large cans work well) and let it drain while the oven preheats.

Slice each block of tofu into ½-inch (1 cm) thick slabs. Place them on the baking sheet in a single layer and lightly coat with cooking spray. In a small bowl, whisk together curry powder, onion powder, salt, and black pepper. Sprinkle half of the spice mix over one side of the tofu and bake for 15 minutes. Flip the tofu, lightly coat with cooking spray, and sprinkle on the remaining of the spice mix. Bake for an additional 15 minutes.

To make the coconut-tahini sauce: While the tofu is baking, whisk the coconut milk, tahini, lime juice, and salt in a small bowl. Refrigerate the sauce until you're ready to assemble the wraps.

To assemble: Divide the coconut-tahini sauce among the wraps, spreading it over the center of each tortilla. Next, place the cabbage, bell pepper, onion, cilantro, and tofu on top of the sauce. Working with one tortilla at a time, wrap up the tortilla by folding two sides of the tortilla toward the center, then rolling the unfolded end closest to you over the filling. Keep rolling until the wrap is completely closed. Serve immediately or store in the refrigerator, wrapped in foil or in an airtight container, for up to 5 days.

YIELD: 5 SERVINGS

NUTRITIONAL ANALYSIS
Per serving: 654 calories; 38 g fat; 45 g carbohydrates; 5 g fiber; 7 g sugar; 30 g protein

Tip!
Make sure that your coconut milk is completely emulsified, or your sauce may be too thin or too thick.

CHIMICHURRI CHICKPEA KALE BOWL

• NEEDS SOME HEAT • 30 MINUTES OR LESS • GLUTEN FREE
• SOY-FREE OPTION • NUT FREE

This meal comes together very easily, but it packs some serious flavor! I *love* using mushrooms in recipes: In combination with chickpeas, they offer a "meaty" base for the bright, acidic chimichurri sauce.

1 cup (200 g) quinoa
2 cups (475 ml) water
2 teaspoons (10 ml) sunflower oil
2 (15-ounce [425 g]) cans chickpeas, drained and rinsed
16 ounces (455 g) cremini or baby bella mushrooms, sliced
2 tablespoons (30 ml) tamari or coconut aminos
1 teaspoon onion powder
¼ teaspoon black pepper
2 tablespoons (30 ml) lime juice
Pinch salt
5 cups (220 g) loosely packed chopped kale
1 batch Chimichurri (page 165)

Rinse quinoa. In a large, covered pot, bring the water and quinoa to a boil over medium heat. Reduce the heat to medium-low and simmer for 15 to 18 minutes. Remove from heat, uncover, and let the cooked quinoa sit for 3 minutes, then fluff it with a fork. Set aside to cool.

While the quinoa is cooking, heat the sunflower oil in a large skillet over medium heat. Add the chickpeas, mushrooms, tamari, onion powder, and pepper and cook until the mushrooms have reduced to nearly half their original size, 5 to 7 minutes. Remove the pan from the heat, stir in lime juice, and add salt to taste.

Divide the kale between 5 bowls or airtight containers, followed by the cooked quinoa and chickpea-mushroom mixture. Top each bowl with Chimichurri. Serve immediately or store in the refrigerator for up to 7 days.

YIELD: 5 SERVINGS

NUTRITIONAL ANALYSIS
Per serving: 440 calories; 16 g fat; 52 g carbohydrates; 11 g fiber; 5 g sugar; 18 g protein

See the Snack Attack! chapter for the Lemon Quinoa Bites (page 144) and Spicy Crusted Kelp Chips (page 147), the snacks listed in this weekly menu.

WEEKLY MENU 2

- *BEGINNER*
- *GLUTEN-FREE OPTION*

Breakfast: **Soyrizo Sheet Pan Hash** (page 24)
Lunch: **Peanutty Tempeh Banh Mi** (page 25)
Dinner: **Lemon-Rosemary Chickpea Pasta Casserole** (page 27)
Snacks: **Apples with Tahini Caramel** (page 154)

SHOPPING LIST

Produce
- ☐ 1½ pounds (680 g) russet potatoes
- ☐ 6 ounces (170 g) baby bella or cremini mushrooms
- ☐ 3 celery stalks
- ☐ 2 carrots
- ☐ 1 small daikon radish
- ☐ 1 small cucumber
- ☐ 1 green bell pepper
- ☐ 1 red bell pepper
- ☐ 1 small jalapeño
- ☐ 1 bunch cilantro
- ☐ 1 small container fresh basil or Thai basil
- ☐ 1 red onion
- ☐ 1 yellow onion
- ☐ 1 head garlic
- ☐ 4 pink apples, or preferred type
- ☐ 1 avocado
- ☐ 3 lemons
- ☐ 1 lime

Refrigerator
- ☐ 2 (8 ounce [225 g]) packages gluten-free tempeh
- ☐ 11-ounce (310 g) package soyrizo (vegan chorizo)
- ☐ 1 small jar vegan mayo

Grocery
- ☐ 5 hoagie-style sandwich buns or 2 baguettes
- ☐ 1 package bowtie pasta
- ☐ 1 quart (950 ml) vegetable broth
- ☐ 2 (15-ounce [425 g]) cans chickpeas
- ☐ 1 small jar creamy peanut butter
- ☐ 1 jar/container tahini
- ☐ 1 bottle tamari
- ☐ 1 bottle sambal oelek chili paste
- ☐ 1 bottle sunflower oil
- ☐ 1 bottle unseasoned rice vinegar
- ☐ 1 small bottle maple syrup

- ☐ 1 small bottle agave nectar
- ☐ 1 small bottle vanilla extract
- ☐ 1 package dried dates

Bulk
- ☐ 1 cup (137 g) raw cashews

Dried Herbs and Spices
- ☐ Dried rosemary
- ☐ Dried oregano
- ☐ Salt
- ☐ Black pepper

GUIDELINES FOR PREPPING

Step 1: Make the Soyrizo Sheet Pan Hash. While it's roasting, you'll have a solid amount of time to make and store the Peanutty Tempeh Banh Mi.

Step 2: Once the hash has roasted, move the baking sheet to a cooling rack, adjust the oven temperature to 375°F (190°C, or gas mark 5), and start the Lemon-Rosemary Chickpea Pasta Casserole. While the casserole bakes, make and store the Apples with Tahini Caramel.

Step 3: Allow the hash and the casserole to cool, then store both in the refrigerator.

SOYRIZO SHEET PAN HASH

- *NEEDS SOME HEAT* • *FREEZER FRIENDLY*
- *GLUTEN FREE* • *NUT FREE* • *NO SUGAR ADDED*

Can I admit something here? Sometimes, I am just plain bad at making hash. Clearly, I have an issue with patience, because I can never wait long enough for the potatoes to brown before moving them around. With this sheet pan hash, I don't have to worry about it; plus, it makes way more than you could fit in a single skillet.

1½ pounds (680 g) russet or Yukon Gold potatoes, diced into ¼-inch (6 mm) pieces

6 ounces (170 g) baby bella or cremini mushrooms, stemmed and diced

1 red onion, diced

1 green bell pepper, diced

1 red bell pepper, diced

½ teaspoon dried oregano

1 (11 ounce [310 g]) package soyrizo

1 avocado

1 lime

If you can't find soyrizo in stores near you, try substituting roughly 11 ounces (310 g) of vegan grounds plus 1 tablespoon (15 ml) organic sunflower oil and 2 teaspoons (5 g) chili powder.

Preheat the oven to 450°F (230°C, or gas mark 8) and line a baking sheet with parchment paper. In a very large bowl, combine the potatoes, mushrooms, onion, bell peppers, and oregano. Squeeze the soyrizo into the bowl and mix using your clean hands, making sure that the soyrizo evenly coats all of the veggies.

Spread the mixture in an even layer on the baking sheet and roast until the potatoes are cooked through, about 50 minutes, stirring halfway through roasting. Move the baking sheet to a rack and let cool for 5 minutes before dividing up between 5 plates or 5 airtight containers. If serving the hash right away, slice the avocado and the lime, divide the avocado evenly among the plates and garnish each plate with a lime wedge. If storing the hash, slice the avocado and lime just before serving. The hash can be stored in the refrigerator for up to 7 days or in the freezer for up to 3 months.

YIELD: 5 SERVINGS

NUTRITIONAL ANALYSIS
Per serving: 359 calories; 10 g fat; 58 g carbohydrates; 11 g fiber; 7 g sugar; 15 g protein

Tip!
Save those odds and ends from the onion and the mushroom stems to use in the Vegetable Scrap Broth (page 165).

PEANUTTY TEMPEH BANH MI

• FRESH OUTTA THE FRIDGE • 30 MINUTES OR LESS • GLUTEN-FREE OPTION

Tip! If you can't find daikon radish, thinly sliced red radishes will also work, though they are a little more peppery.

There's a huge Vietnamese population in the county where I've spent most of my life, and I'm lucky to have eaten so much Vietnamese food over the years. One tried-and-true dish that I'll order almost any time I see it on a menu is Banh Mi. Pickled veggies, fresh herbs, spicy jalapeños, and a savory, protein-rich filling? Yes, please!

FOR THE VEGGIES:
2 tablespoons (30 ml) unseasoned rice vinegar
2 teaspoons (10 ml) agave nectar
¼ teaspoon salt
1 cup (116 g) peeled and thinly sliced daikon radish
1 cup (119 g) peeled and thinly sliced cucumber
1 cup (130 g) peeled and thinly sliced carrot

FOR THE TEMPEH:
1 cup (235 ml) water
2 (8 ounce [225 g]) packages gluten-free tempeh
¼ cup (65 g) natural smooth peanut butter
2 tablespoons (30 ml) unseasoned rice vinegar
1½ tablespoons (25 ml) tamari
1 tablespoon (10 g) sambal oelek chili paste
1 tablespoon (15 ml) agave nectar

FOR THE ASSEMBLY:
5 hoagie-style sandwich buns or 2 baguettes, gluten-free if desired
5 tablespoons (60 g) vegan mayo or Gochujang Aioli (page 161)
¼ cup (4 g) cilantro leaves
¼ cup (6 g) basil or Thai basil leaves
1 small jalapeño, sliced (optional)

To make the veggies: In a medium bowl, whisk together the rice vinegar, agave, and salt. Add the daikon, cucumber, and carrot and toss until the veggies are coated. Refrigerate the mixture until you're ready to assemble the sandwiches.

To make the tempeh: In a large sauté pan, bring the water to a simmer over medium-low heat. Cut the tempeh into 8 equal slabs and place them in the simmering water. Cover the pan with a lid and simmer the tempeh for 5 minutes to get rid of its bitterness. Transfer the tempeh to a cutting board and slice it into ½-inch (1 cm) thick strips. Drain the water from the pan.

In a large bowl, whisk together the peanut butter, rice vinegar, tamari, chili paste, and agave nectar until smooth. Add the tempeh and toss gently to coat in sauce. Add half of the mixture to the now-empty pan and cook over medium-low heat until warmed through, about 5 minutes. Transfer the cooked tempeh to a bowl and repeat with the remaining tempeh mixture.

To assemble: Slice the rolls in half lengthwise, leaving one side uncut for a hinge. Spread each roll with 1 tablespoon of the mayo, then layer on the tempeh and pickled veggies. Divide the basil and cilantro evenly among the sandwiches. Serve immediately or store in the refrigerator, wrapped in foil or in an airtight container, for up to 5 days.

YIELD: 5 SERVINGS

NUTRITIONAL ANALYSIS
Per serving: 495 calories; 20 g fat; 52 g carbohydrates; 8 g fiber; 18 g sugar; 31 g protein

LEMON-ROSEMARY CHICKPEA PASTA CASSEROLE

- **NEEDS SOME HEAT** - **FREEZER FRIENDLY** - **GLUTEN-FREE OPTION**
- **SOY FREE** - **NO SUGAR ADDED**

I almost never make pasta casseroles—with the exception of mac and cheese—but this recipe has me asking myself, "Why the heck not?" Easy to prepare, lemony, herby, and downright comforting, this chickpea and pasta casserole delivers on all fronts!

See the Snack Attack! chapter for the Apples with Tahini Caramel (page 154), the snack in this week's menu.

2 teaspoons (10 ml) sunflower oil

1 cup (140 g) diced yellow onion

1 cup (130 g) diced carrot

1 cup (100 g) diced celery

2 (15-ounce [425 g]) cans chickpeas, drained, with 1 cup (235 ml) liquid reserved

1 cup (137 g) raw cashews

¼ cup (60 ml) lemon juice plus 1 tablespoon (6 g) zest

3 cloves garlic, peeled

2 teaspoons (2 g) dried rosemary

1 teaspoon salt

½ teaspoon black pepper

4 cups (280 g) bowtie pasta, gluten-free if desired

4 cups (950 ml) hot vegetable broth or vegan chicken broth

Preheat oven to 375°F (190°C, or gas mark 5). In a large skillet, heat the oil over medium heat. Add the onion, carrot, and celery and cook until the onions are close to translucent, about 5 minutes. Add the chickpeas and cook for another 2 minutes.

While the veggie mixture is cooking, puree the chickpea liquid, cashews, lemon juice and zest, garlic, rosemary, salt, and pepper in a blender until very smooth. Let sit for 2 minutes, then blend again.

Pour the pasta, hot broth, chickpea mixture, and blended sauce into a 9 x 13-inch (23 x 33 cm) casserole dish. Stir to combine and spread mixture into an even layer. Cover the dish with foil and bake for 30 minutes. Carefully remove the foil and bake until the pasta is cooked through and the sauce is no longer runny, about 10 minutes longer. Let cool on a rack for 15 minutes before serving. Casserole can be stored in the refrigerator for up to 7 days or in the freezer for up to 3 months.

YIELD: 5 SERVINGS

NUTRITIONAL ANALYSIS
Per serving: 510 calories; 13 g fat; 75 g carbohydrates; 14 g fiber; 9 g sugar; 20 g protein

Tip! Save those odds and ends from the onions, celery, and carrots to use in the Vegetable Scrap Broth (page 165).

Note: If you want to dress this dish up looks-wise, top it with a few sprigs of rosemary during the last 10 minutes of baking.

WEEKLY MENU 3

- **BEGINNER**
- **GLUTEN-FREE OPTION**
- **SOY FREE**

Breakfast: **Blueberry Jar Smoothies** (page 30)
Lunch: **Southwest Salad** (page 31)
Dinner: **Smoky Sweet Potato Soup** (page 32)
Snacks: **Pizza Kale Chips** (page 152) and
    Chocolate Peanut Butter Rice Bars (page 153)

SHOPPING LIST

Produce

- ☐ 1½ pounds (680 g) romaine lettuce
- ☐ 1 bunch (roughly 12 ounces or 340 g) curly kale
- ☐ 1½ pounds (680 g) sweet potatoes
- ☐ 2 large carrots
- ☐ 2 orange bell peppers
- ☐ 1 yellow bell pepper
- ☐ 1 jalapeño
- ☐ 1 large red onion
- ☐ 1 head garlic
- ☐ 1 container grape tomatoes
- ☐ 1 bunch radishes
- ☐ 1 avocado
- ☐ 5 small bananas
- ☐ 1 bunch fresh cilantro
- ☐ 2 limes
- ☐ 1 lemon

Grocery

- ☐ 6-ounce (170 g) can tomato paste
- ☐ 1 quart (950 ml) vegetable broth
- ☐ 8-ounce (225 g) bag hemp hearts
- ☐ 1 small bag ground flaxseed
- ☐ 1 bottle olive oil
- ☐ 1 bottle sunflower oil
- ☐ 1 jar refined coconut oil
- ☐ 1 box brown rice crisps cereal
- ☐ 1 small jar creamy peanut butter
- ☐ 9-ounce (255 g) bag vegan chocolate chips
- ☐ 1 small bottle agave nectar
- ☐ 1 small boule or loaf of crusty bread such as sourdough, gluten-free if desired (optional)

Frozen

- ☐ 2 (16-ounce [455 g]) bags frozen chopped spinach
- ☐ 3 (12-ounce [340 g]) bags frozen blueberries
- ☐ 2 (16-ounce [455 g]) bags frozen pineapple chunks

Bulk

- ☐ 12 ounces (340 g) red quinoa
- ☐ ½ cup (70 g) roasted pumpkin seeds (pepitas)
- ☐ ¾ cup (103 g) raw cashews
- ☐ ½ cup (73 g) roasted peanuts

Dried Herbs and Spices

- ☐ Ground turmeric
- ☐ Ground ginger
- ☐ Ground cumin
- ☐ Smoked paprika
- ☐ Garlic powder
- ☐ Onion powder
- ☐ Cayenne pepper
- ☐ Dried oregano
- ☐ Dried basil
- ☐ Crushed red pepper (optional)
- ☐ Nutritional yeast
- ☐ Vanilla extract
- ☐ Salt
- ☐ Coarse salt for sprinkling

GUIDELINES FOR PREPPING

Step 1: Preheat the oven to 350°F (180°C, or gas mark 4), and prepare the Pizza Kale Chips. While the chips are baking, assemble and refrigerate the Chocolate Peanut Butter Rice Bars.

Step 2: While the chips are cooling and the bars are chilling, assemble and freeze the Blueberry Smoothie Jars. Once the chips have cooled, store them, then finish the prep on the bars and store them in the refrigerator.

Step 3: Start on the Smoky Sweet Potato Soup. While it simmers, make and store the Cilantro Jalapeño Cashew Dressing for the Southwest Salad. Finish making and storing the soup.

Step 4: Prep, assemble, and store the Southwest Salads.

BLUEBERRY SMOOTHIE JARS

• *FREEZER FRIENDLY* • *30 MINUTES OR LESS* • *UNDER 10 INGREDIENTS*
• *GLUTEN FREE* • *SOY FREE* • *NUT FREE* • *OIL FREE* • *NO SUGAR ADDED*

Smoothie jars make getting out the door during the week so much easier. This recipe is the base version of my favorite—and most commonly made—smoothie, because blueberries and pineapple are so dreamy together. I've ordered the ingredients in the recipe to make the smoothies easy to blend. I like keeping bananas at room temperature so that each morning I can add one to the blender pitcher before dumping the jar contents on top.

2½ cups (265 g) frozen chopped spinach, broken into pieces

4 cups (560 g) frozen blueberries

2½ cups (365 g) frozen pineapple chunks

1 cup (150 g) hemp hearts

1¼ teaspoons ground turmeric

1¼ teaspoons ground ginger

5 small bananas

3¾ cups (890 ml) water

Set out five 24-ounce (710 ml) wide mouth jars. Divide the spinach, blueberries, pineapple, hemp hearts, turmeric, and ginger evenly among the jars; screw the lids on the jars and store in the freezer.

When you're ready to make a smoothie, add one peeled banana, broken into chunks, to the blender. Run warm water over the outside of one covered jar to help release the frozen ingredients. Pour the jar contents into the blender, followed by ¾ cup (175 ml) water. Blend until completely smooth, then transfer back to the jar and enjoy.

YIELD: 5 SERVINGS

NUTRITIONAL ANALYSIS
Per serving: 410 calories; 15 g fat; 57 g carbohydrates; 11 g fiber; 35 g sugar; 14 g protein

Smoothies are highly customizable, so try this recipe as-is first, then swap in your favorite fruits, spices, or proteins for different versions. During the summer, I like to substitute half of the banana for peach slices.

SOUTHWEST SALAD

• FRESH OUTTA THE FRIDGE • 30 MINUTES OR LESS • GLUTEN FREE • SOY FREE • NUT FREE • OIL FREE • NO SUGAR ADDED

Over the last few years, I've made various versions of this salad, but this version has the most beautiful colors and texture. It's crunchy, fresh, and bright, and the Cilantro Jalapeño Cashew Dressing (page 161) is the perfect creamy, tangy topping.

1½ pounds (680 g) romaine lettuce, chopped

2 (15-ounce [425 g]) cans low-sodium black beans, drained and rinsed

1 yellow bell pepper, stemmed, seeded, and diced

1 orange bell pepper, stemmed, seeded, and diced

1¼ cups (188 g) grape tomatoes

⅔ cup (110 g) thinly sliced red onion

⅔ cup (95 g) sliced radishes

⅔ cup (60 g) sliced avocado

1 batch Cilantro Jalapeño Cashew Dressing (page 161)

Set out five roughly 30-ounce (850 g) storage containers. Divide the lettuce evenly among the containers, then top with black beans, bell peppers, tomatoes, and onion. Top each serving with radishes and sliced avocado.

Drizzle the dressing over the top of each salad (or divide into five small containers or jars). Store in the refrigerator for up to 6 days.

YIELD: 5 SERVINGS

NUTRITIONAL ANALYSIS
Per serving (including dressing): 248 calories; 11 g fat; 31 g carbohydrates; 10 g fiber; 11 g sugar; 10 g protein

See the Snack Attack! chapter for the Pizza Kale Chips (page 152) and Chocolate Peanut Butter Rice Bars (page 153), the snacks listed in this weekly menu.

SMOKY SWEET POTATO SOUP

• NEEDS SOME HEAT • FREEZER FRIENDLY • GLUTEN FREE
• SOY FREE • NUT FREE • NO SUGAR ADDED

When I first went vegan, I subscribed to a Community Supported Agriculture (CSA) box, and the company that ran it would send recipe suggestions with each delivery. This played a huge part in my learning how to cook! A recipe similar to this one came to me with a ton of sweet potatoes, and after some serious tweaking I think it has reached its full potential. Smoky but not overly so, a little sweet but still savory, and super-satiating. Though the toasted bread is optional, I love eating this soup with a crusty slice of sourdough.

1 tablespoon (15 ml) sun-
flower oil

1½ cups (190 g) diced red
onion

1¼ cups (188 g) diced orange
bell pepper

1½ pounds (680 g) sweet
potatoes, unpeeled, diced

2 large carrots, chopped

3 cloves garlic, minced

2 tablespoons (10 g) nutritional yeast

2 teaspoons (5 g) smoked
paprika

1 teaspoon garlic powder

1 teaspoon ground cumin

4 cups (950 ml) vegetable
broth

2 cups (475 ml) water

⅔ cup (116 g) red quinoa,
rinsed

1 cup (110 g) frozen spinach,
broken up into pieces

½–1 teaspoon salt

½ cup (70 g) roasted pumpkin seeds (pepitas)

¼ cup (4 g) fresh cilantro
leaves

5 slices of toasted crusty
bread (optional)

In a large pot, heat the sunflower oil over medium heat. Add the red onion and bell pepper and cook, stirring frequently, until the onion is softened, about 5 minutes. Adjust the heat to medium-low and add the sweet potatoes, carrots, garlic, nutritional yeast, smoked paprika, garlic powder, and cumin. Cook for 5 more minutes, adding 1 or 2 tablespoons (15 to 30 ml) water if necessary to prevent sticking.

Stir in the vegetable broth, water, and quinoa, cover, and bring to a boil over medium-high heat. Once boiling, adjust the heat so that the soup is simmering, cover, and cook, stirring occasionally, until the quinoa is tender, about 20 minutes longer.

Puree half of the soup mixture using an immersion blender or by carefully transferring to a blender. Add the spinach, stirring to break up any clumps, and add salt to taste. Let the soup cool for 20 minutes, then divide it between 5 jars or storage containers. Top each serving with the pumpkin seeds and cilantro and store in the refrigerator for up to 7 days. Serve with a slice of bread, if desired.

YIELD: 5 SERVINGS

NUTRITIONAL ANALYSIS
Per serving (not including bread): 427 calories; 11 g fat; 72 g carbohydrates; 13 g fiber; 17 g sugar; 13 g protein

Tip!
Save those odds and ends from the red onion and carrots to use in the Vegetable Scrap Broth (page 165)!

This soup is great for storing in the fridge to eat during the week, and it also freezes well if you want to plan way ahead. If you choose to freeze it, divide it into five freezer-safe storage containers and freeze for up to 6 months.

WEEKLY MENU 4

- *BEGINNER*
- *GLUTEN-FREE*
- *SOY-FREE OPTION*

Breakfast: **Minty Peach Yogurt Bowls** (page 36)
Lunch: **Summer Veggie–Stuffed Potatoes** (page 37)
Dinner: **Jackfruit Tacos with Black Beans** (page 39)
Snacks: **Grain-Free Granola** (page 149)

SHOPPING LIST

Produce

- ☐ 5 large russet potatoes, roughly 5 inches (13 cm) long
- ☐ 1 small head of green cabbage or package of shredded cabbage
- ☐ 1 large carrot
- ☐ 2 radishes
- ☐ 1 pound (455 g) yellow squash
- ☐ 8 ounces (225 g) zucchini
- ☐ 4 ounces (115 g) green beans
- ☐ 1 small container cherry tomatoes
- ☐ 1 red onion
- ☐ 1 small white onion
- ☐ 1 small package fresh basil
- ☐ 1 bunch fresh cilantro
- ☐ 1 small package mint
- ☐ 2 limes
- ☐ 16 ounces (455 g) peaches, fresh or frozen

Grocery

- ☐ 2 (15-ounce [425 g]) cans low-sodium black beans
- ☐ 3 (14-ounce [400 g]) cans young jackfruit in brine
- ☐ 10 small corn tortillas
- ☐ 1 bottle tamari or coconut aminos
- ☐ 1 jar smooth almond butter
- ☐ 1 bottle sunflower oil
- ☐ 1 box brown rice crisp cereal
- ☐ 1 bag arrowroot starch
- ☐ 1 bottle maple syrup
- ☐ 1 package dried dates

Refrigerator

- ☐ 2 (24-ounce [680 g]) containers plain nondairy yogurt
- ☐ 1 jar vegan kimchi

Freezer

- ☐ 1 small package frozen corn

Bulk

- ☐ 1 cup (123 g) roasted pistachios
- ☐ 1 cup (137 g) raw cashews
- ☐ ¾ cup (109 g) almonds
- ☐ 1 cup (140 g) raw pumpkin seeds (pepitas)
- ☐ ½ cup (73 g) sunflower seeds
- ☐ ¼ cup (44 g) chia seeds
- ☐ ¾ cup (45 g) unsweetened coconut flakes

Dried Herbs and Spices

- ☐ Ancho chile powder (or chili powder)
- ☐ Dried oregano
- ☐ Onion powder
- ☐ Garlic powder
- ☐ Ground cumin
- ☐ Ground cinnamon
- ☐ Bay leaves
- ☐ Vanilla extract
- ☐ Nutritional yeast
- ☐ Salt

GUIDELINES FOR PREPPING

Step 1: Make the Grain-Free Granola. While it's baking, cook the potatoes for the Summer Veggie–Stuffed Potatoes in a multicooker or pressure cooker. While the potatoes are cooking, make and store the Kimchi Cheese Sauce for the potatoes.

Step 2: While the granola is cooling, finish making the stuffed potato filling, then assemble and store the potatoes.

Step 3: Start the Jackfruit Tacos with Black Beans. While the jackfruit and beans are cooking, assemble and store the Minty Peach Yogurt Bowls. Once the tacos are complete, assemble and store them. When the granola is cool, store that as well.

MINTY PEACH YOGURT BOWL

• FRESH OUTTA THE FRIDGE • 30 MINUTES OR LESS
• UNDER 10 INGREDIENTS • GLUTEN FREE • SOY FREE

Eating yogurt for breakfast seems like a pretty obvious suggestion, but believe me, with a little help from some fresh ingredients it gets so much better! I used peaches and mint here, but another good combination is strawberries and basil.

48 ounces (1360 g) plain nondairy yogurt

¼ cup (60 ml) maple syrup

3 tablespoons (18 g) minced fresh mint

2 teaspoons (10 ml) vanilla extract

5 cups (405 g) chopped peaches (fresh or thawed frozen)

1 cup (123 g) roasted pistachios

2½ cups (90 g) brown rice crisps cereal

In a medium bowl, stir together the yogurt, maple syrup, mint, and vanilla until combined. Divide the mixture between 5 bowls or jars, then top with peaches and pistachios. Top each bowl with ½ cup (18 g) cereal just before serving. Yogurt bowls can be stored in the refrigerator for up to 5 days.

YIELD: 5 SERVINGS

NUTRITIONAL ANALYSIS
Per serving: 419 calories; 19 g fat; 60 g carbohydrates; 4 g fiber; 26 g sugar; 10 g protein

Have a few minutes to spare? Top your yogurt with the Stovetop Granola from my Protein Smoothie Bowl (page 108) instead of the brown rice crisps.

See the Snack Attack! chapter for the Grain-Free Granola (page 149), the snack listed in this weekly menu.

SUMMER VEGGIE–STUFFED POTATOES

• NEEDS SOME HEAT • GLUTEN FREE • SOY FREE • NO SUGAR ADDED

Baked potatoes aren't just for stuffing with heavy, dairy-filled condiments: They're like an edible canvas that you can top with nearly anything! I've loaded up these potatoes with sautéed summer veggies and fresh basil, along with my amazing Kimchi Cheese Sauce (page 158).

5 large russet potatoes, roughly 5 inches (13 cm) long

2 teaspoons sunflower oil

1 cup (140 g) diced red onion

1 pound (455 g) yellow squash, quartered length-wise and sliced

8 ounces (225 g) zucchini, quartered lengthwise and sliced

1 cup (100 g) chopped fresh green beans

1½ cups (245 g) halved cherry tomatoes

1 cup (180 g) frozen corn, thawed

2 tablespoons (5 g) minced fresh basil, divided

½ teaspoon salt

1 batch Kimchi Cheese Sauce (page 158)

Pierce each potato four times with a fork, then place the potatoes on a rack in a 6-quart Instant Pot or pressure cooker. Add 1 cup water to the pot, then bring to high pressure. When the pot reaches full pressure, cook for 17 minutes. Allow the covered pot to cool for 5 minutes before quick-releasing the pressure. (See Tip, below, if you do not have a pressure cooker.)

While the potatoes are cooking, heat the oil in a large skillet over medium heat. Add the onion and cook until starting to soften, 2 to 3 minutes. Add the yellow squash, zucchini, and green beans and cook until the squashes are tender, 7 to 10 minutes. Add the tomatoes and corn and cook for 3 minutes, then stir in 1 tablespoon (2 g) of the basil and the salt and cook for 1 minute longer. Season with salt to taste, remove the pan from the heat, and cover to keep warm.

Slice each potato down the middle (don't go all the way through) and squeeze the ends together to open up the cuts. Divide the veggie mixture evenly among the potatoes. Just before serving, warm the Kimchi Cheese Sauce over medium heat until it's bubbling and the starch has activated, about 5 minutes, then pour over the potatoes and sprinkle with basil. The potatoes and sauce can be stored in the refrigerator separately for up to 7 days.

YIELD: 5 SERVINGS

NUTRITIONAL ANALYSIS
Per serving: 536 calories; 13 g fat; 90 g carbohydrates; 12 g fiber; 15 g sugar; 17 g protein

Tip!
If you do not have a pressure cooker, preheat the oven to 425°F (220°C, or gas mark 7) and pierce each potato four times with a fork. Wrap each one in foil and bake until they are tender when poked with a fork, 45 to 50 minutes.

JACKFRUIT TACOS WITH BLACK BEANS

• NEEDS SOME HEAT • 30 MINUTES OR LESS • GLUTEN-FREE
• SOY FREE OPTION • NUT FREE • NO SUGAR ADDED

California has the best and most accessible Mexican food outside of Mexico, hands down, which meant growing up in Southern California had some serious food perks. These tacos are reminiscent of the street tacos from the food trucks I would ride my bike to. Of course, I had to round them out with a side of seasoned black beans!

FOR THE TACOS:
3 (14-ounce [400 g]) cans young jackfruit in brine, drained, rinsed, and seeded
1 tablespoon (15 ml) sunflower oil
1½ teaspoons ancho chile powder
1 teaspoon dried oregano
½ teaspoon onion powder
¼ cup (60 ml) water
1½ tablespoons (25 ml) tamari or coconut aminos
1 tablespoon (15 ml) maple syrup

FOR THE BEANS:
2 (15-ounce [425 g]) cans low-sodium black beans, liquid reserved
3 bay leaves
1 teaspoon ground cumin
1 teaspoon onion powder
½ teaspoon garlic powder
¼ to ½ teaspoon salt

FOR THE ASSEMBLY:
10 small corn tortillas
1½ cups (118 g) shredded green cabbage
½ cup (70 g) diced white onion
¼ cup (4 g) chopped cilantro, loosely packed
2 radishes, quartered and sliced thin
5 lime wedges

To make the tacos: Pull apart any large pieces of jackfruit. In a large skillet, heat the oil over medium heat. Add the jackfruit, ancho chile powder, oregano, and onion powder and cook until the jackfruit is browned and dry and the edges are crispy, 5 to 7 minutes.

Add the water, tamari, and maple syrup and continue to cook until the liquid has been soaked up and the edges of the jackfruit start to sizzle. Turn heat to low to keep warm (or remove from heat if storing).

To make the beans: While the jackfruit is cooking, simmer the beans and their liquid, the bay leaves, cumin, onion powder, garlic powder, and salt over medium-low heat, with vented lid, until warmed through, about 10 minutes. Remove and discard the bay leaves.

To assemble: Divide the beans among 5 small storage containers (or the small sections of five partitioned storage containers). Warm the tortillas by toasting them one at a time over a gas burner or microwaving the stack for 30 seconds. Place 2 tortillas in each of 5 large storage containers (or the large section of the partitioned containers), and divide jackfruit evenly among tortillas. Top jackfruit with cabbage, onion, cilantro, and radishes and place lime wedges on the side. Tacos can be stored in the refrigerator for up to 5 days.

YIELD: 5 SERVINGS

NUTRITIONAL ANALYSIS
Per serving: 415 calories; 5 g fat; 81 g carbohydrates; 34 g fiber; 6 g sugar; 19 g protein

WEEKLY MENU 5

- **BEGINNER**
- **NUT-FREE OPTION**

Breakfast: **Breakfast Sandwiches** (page 42)
Lunch: **Asparagus Orzo Salad** (page 43)
Dinner: **Naked Seitan Piccata** (page 45)
Snacks: **Almond Cranberry Bark** (page 150)

SHOPPING LIST

Produce

- ☐ 4 cups (120 g) baby arugula
- ☐ 2½ cups (56 g) mixed greens or baby spinach
- ☐ 1 tomato
- ☐ 1 pound (455 g) asparagus
- ☐ 1 pound (455 g) summer squash or zucchini
- ☐ 1 small bunch radishes
- ☐ 1 yellow onion
- ☐ 3 shallots
- ☐ 1 head garlic
- ☐ 1 bunch green onions
- ☐ 1 bunch fresh dill
- ☐ 1 bunch fresh parsley
- ☐ 5 lemons

Grocery

- ☐ 2 quarts (1.9 L) vegetable broth
- ☐ 6-ounce (170 g) can tomato paste
- ☐ 1 jar capers
- ☐ 1 package orzo, gluten free if desired
- ☐ 1 package vegan English muffins, gluten free if desired
- ☐ 1 package brown rice flour
- ☐ 1 package tapioca flour
- ☐ 1 container vital wheat gluten
- ☐ 1 bag unsweetened coconut flakes
- ☐ 2 (9-ounce [255 g]) bags vegan chocolate chips
- ☐ 1 package dried cranberries
- ☐ 1 bottle sunflower oil
- ☐ 1 jar refined coconut oil
- ☐ 1 bottle olive oil

Refrigerator

- ☐ 1 (14-ounce [395 g]) package extra-firm tofu
- ☐ 1 jar vegan mayo
- ☐ 1 container vegan butter
- ☐ 1 package vegan cheese slices (optional)

Freezer

- ☐ 1 bag frozen peas

Bulk

- ☐ 1½ cups (218 g) raw almonds
- ☐ ¾ cup (105 g) pine nuts or sunflower seeds

Dried Herbs and Spices

- ☐ Onion powder
- ☐ Smoked paprika
- ☐ Salt-free poultry seasoning
- ☐ Ground turmeric
- ☐ Nutritional yeast
- ☐ *Kala namak* (Indian black salt)
- ☐ Coarse salt
- ☐ Salt

GUIDELINES FOR PREPPING

Step 1: Start the Seitan Cutlets. While they are simmering, make and freeze the Almond Cranberry Bark. Once the seitan is done simmering, drain the broth and store the cutlets in the refrigerator until you're ready to make the Naked Seitan Piccata.

Step 2: Start cooking the orzo. While it's boiling, coat the tofu for the Breakfast Sandwiches. Once the orzo is cooked, drain and rinse it. While it cools, finish making the breakfast sandwiches.

Step 3: Make the rest of the Asparagus Orzo Salad components, then assemble and store the salads. Lastly, make and store the Naked Seitan Piccata.

BREAKFAST SANDWICHES

• FRESH OUTTA THE FRIDGE • 30 MINUTES OR LESS
• GLUTEN-FREE OPTION • NUT FREE • NO SUGAR ADDED

English muffin? Check. Eggy tofu? Check. Some fresh ingredients and a slice of vegan cheese? Check and check. Looks like we have everything we need for an awesome start to the day!

1 (14-ounce [395 g]) package extra-firm tofu, drained

3 tablespoons (21 g) Vegan Eggy Seasoning (page 169)

2 tablespoons (20 g) brown rice flour

2 teaspoons sunflower oil

Salt

5 vegan English muffins, gluten free if desired, toasted

5 tablespoons (75 g) vegan mayo

5 slices vegan cheese (optional)

2½ cups (56 g) loosely packed mixed greens or baby spinach

½ cup (90 g) thinly sliced tomato, seeded

Slice the tofu widthwise into 10 slabs and set them on a clean kitchen towel or paper towel to drain. In a shallow bowl or plate, combine the Vegan Eggy Seasoning and rice flour. Place one piece of tofu in the flour mixture and turn to coat all sides. Set aside. Repeat with remaining tofu.

Heat a large skillet or griddle over medium heat and brush on the sunflower oil. Cook the tofu until crispy on both sides, 2 to 3 minutes, flipping halfway through cooking. Remove the skillet from the heat.

To assemble the sandwiches, spread each English muffin half with ½ table-spoon vegan mayo. Place 2 pieces of tofu on each muffin base, followed by cheese, if using, mixed greens, and tomato. Top with remaining halves of the English muffins. Breakfast sandwiches can be wrapped in paper and stored in the refrigerator for up to 5 days; you can eat them straight from the fridge or reheat them in the microwave or toaster oven.

YIELD: 5 SERVINGS

NUTRITIONAL ANALYSIS
Per serving: 384 calories; 16 g fat; 40 g carbohydrates; 8 g fiber; 3 g sugar; 20 g protein

ASPARAGUS ORZO SALAD

• FRESH OUTTA THE FRIDGE • 30 MINUTES OR LESS
• GLUTEN-FREE OPTION • NUT-FREE OPTION • NO SUGAR ADDED

This Asparagus Orzo Salad screams spring! Instead of blanching the asparagus, I sauté it to add another layer of flavor to the fresh herbs and bright lemon juice. If you're looking for an easy-to-make, mood-lifting dish, this one is perfect.

2 cups (320 g) orzo, gluten free if desired

2 teaspoons sunflower oil

8 ounces (225 g) asparagus, woody ends removed, chopped

2 cups (310 g) frozen peas, thawed

¾ cup (105 g) pine nuts or sunflower seeds

4 cups (120 g) firmly packed baby arugula

½ cup (58 g) sliced radishes

¼ cup (25 g) diced green onion

¼ to ⅓ cup (60 to 80 ml) lemon juice

2 tablespoons (5 g) chopped dill

2 tablespoons (8 g) chopped parsley

1 tablespoon (15 ml) olive oil (optional)

½ teaspoon salt

¼ teaspoon black pepper

Prepare the orzo according to the package instructions; when just past al dente, drain and rinse with cold water. Set aside to fully cool. While the orzo is cooking, heat the sunflower oil in a large skillet over medium heat. Add the asparagus and cook until it begins to brown, 5 to 7 minutes.

Add the peas and the pine nuts to the pan and cook, stirring often, until the nuts are toasted and golden in color, 1 to 2 minutes. Transfer the asparagus mixture to a large bowl and let cool to room temperature. Add the cooled orzo and the arugula, radishes, green onion, lemon juice, dill, parsley, and olive oil, if using, to the bowl. Season with the salt and pepper and chill for 10 minutes before serving. Salad can be stored in the refrigerator for up to 7 days.

YIELD: 5 SERVINGS

NUTRITIONAL ANALYSIS
Per serving (without olive oil): 519 calories; 18 g fat; 76 g carbohydrates; 10 g fiber; 13 g sugar; 19 g protein

See the Snack Attack! chapter for the Almond Cranberry Bark (page 150), the snack listed in this weekly menu.

NAKED SEITAN PICCATA

- *NEEDS SOME HEAT* • *FREEZER FRIENDLY* • *SOY-FREE OPTION*
- *NUT FREE* • *NO SUGAR ADDED*

While traditional chicken piccata calls for lightly breading the cutlets before frying, that breaded coating just doesn't work when meal prepping: the coating does not hold up when stored in the refrigerator. Hence: naked seitan! It is still mighty tasty, and as a bonus, it's a little easier to make.

FOR THE SEITAN:

2 tablespoons (28 g) vegan butter, soy free if desired, divided

2 tablespoons (30 ml) sunflower oil, divided

1 batch Seitan Cutlets (page 168)

1 tablespoon (8 g) unbleached all-purpose flour

1 cup (235 ml) vegetable broth

¼ cup (60 ml) lemon juice

2 tablespoons (27 g) capers, with brine

2 tablespoons (8 g) chopped parsley, divided

Salt

Black pepper

FOR THE VEGETABLES:

2 teaspoons sunflower oil

3 large shallots, sliced

8 ounces (225 g) asparagus, woody ends removed, chopped

4 cups (420 g) halved and sliced summer squash or zucchini

Salt

Black pepper

Tip!
If you have an air fryer, use it to reheat the Seitan Cutlets throughout the week. Try air frying at 375°F (190°C) for 5 to 7 minutes to warm it all the way through.

To make the seitan: In a large skillet, heat 1 tablespoon (14 g) vegan butter and 1 tablespoon (15 ml) oil over medium heat. Add half of the Seitan Cutlets and fry until lightly golden, 2 to 3 minutes, flipping halfway through. This will firm up the outside of the seitan and impart some buttery flavor. Transfer the seitan to a paper towel–lined plate. Repeat with the remaining butter, oil, and Seitan Cutlets.

Adjust the heat to medium-low and add the flour to the leftover oil mixture. Cook until the flour is lightly browned, then whisk in the vegetable broth, lemon juice, and capers with their brine. Bring to a simmer and cook for 10 minutes, whisking occasionally. Once the sauce has reduced a little bit, add 1 tablespoon (4 g) of the fresh parsley, season with salt and pepper, and remove from the heat.

To make the vegetables: While the sauce is cooking, heat the oil in a large skillet over medium heat. Add the shallots and asparagus and cook for 3 minutes. Add the squash and cook until the squash has softened and reduced in size, about 5 minutes longer. Season with salt and pepper. Divide the veggies between 5 plates or airtight containers, top with 2 of the seitan cutlets, and top with the remaining parsley. Drizzle with the caper sauce just before serving. Veggie/seitan mixture and sauce can be stored separately in the refrigerator for up to 7 days or in the freezer for up to 3 months.

YIELD: 5 SERVINGS

NUTRITIONAL ANALYSIS
Per serving: 376 calories; 19 g fat; 24 g carbohydrates; 3 g fiber; 7 g sugar; 30 g protein

WEEKLY MENU 6

- **BEGINNER**
- **GLUTEN-FREE OPTION**
- **SOY FREE**
- **NUT-FREE OPTION**

Breakfast: **Baked Berry Oatmeal** (page 48)
Lunch: **Fajita Pita Pockets** (page 49)
Dinner: **Creamy Avocado Tahini Zoodles** (page 50)
Snacks: **Buckwheat Ginger Balls** (page 141)

SHOPPING LIST

Produce

- ☐ 1 large or 2 small heads romaine lettuce
- ☐ 3 pounds (1.4 kg) zucchini, roughly 8 small squash
- ☐ 2 red bell peppers
- ☐ 2 green bell peppers
- ☐ 2 tomatoes
- ☐ 1 red onion
- ☐ 1 bunch or 1 small package chives
- ☐ 1 bunch flat-leaf parsley
- ☐ 3 avocados
- ☐ 4 cups (600 g) mixed berries (strawberries, blueberries, etc.)
- ☐ 2 lemons
- ☐ 1 lime

Grocery

- ☐ 2 (15-ounce [425 g]) cans chickpeas
- ☐ 2 (15-ounce [425 g]) cans vegan refried beans
- ☐ 1 (13.5-ounce [400 ml]) full-fat coconut milk
- ☐ 5 pitas or gluten-free wraps
- ☐ 1 package dried dates
- ☐ 1 small package raisins or currants
- ☐ 1 small jar Kalamata olives
- ☐ 1 jar tahini
- ☐ 1 bottle sunflower oil
- ☐ 1 bottle maple syrup or agave nectar

Refrigerator

- ☐ 1 container plain unsweetened nondairy milk

Bulk

- ☐ 2 tablespoons (17 g) chia seeds
- ☐ ½ cup (73 g) raw sunflower seeds
- ☐ ⅔ cup (66 g) raw walnut halves or sunflower seeds
- ☐ 2½ cups (230 g) rolled oats
- ☐ 1 cup (164 g) buckwheat groats

Dried Herbs and Spices

- ☐ Garlic powder
- ☐ Ground cumin
- ☐ Ground ginger
- ☐ Vanilla extract
- ☐ Salt
- ☐ Black pepper

GUIDELINES FOR PREPPING

Step 1: Because this menu is really simple, these steps aren't too involved. Start making the Baked Berry Oatmeal. While it is baking, make and store the Fajita Pita Pockets.

Step 2: While the oatmeal is cooling, make and store the Buckwheat Ginger Balls. Next, make and store the Creamy Avocado Tahini Zoodles.

Step 3: Once the oatmeal has cooled, divide it into storage containers, top with the fruit and nuts, and store in the refrigerator.

BAKED BERRY OATMEAL

- FRESH OUTTA THE FRIDGE • FREEZER FRIENDLY
- UNDER 10 INGREDIENTS • GLUTEN-FREE • SOY FREE
- NUT-FREE OPTION • OIL FREE

Even though traditional oatmeal comes together quickly, baked oatmeal has a special place in my heart. I love the "set it and forget" aspect of this recipe, as you just dump everything into one dish, stir it around, and leave it in the oven to take care of itself.

1½ cups (360 ml) warm water

2 tablespoons (17 g) chia seeds

2½ cups (230 g) rolled oats

4 cups (600 g) mixed berries (strawberries, blueberries, etc.), cut into bite-sized pieces if necessary, divided

⅔ cup (66 g) raw walnut halves or sunflower seeds, divided

1 cup (235 ml) plain unsweet-ened nondairy milk

⅓ cup (80 ml) maple syrup or agave nectar

2 teaspoons vanilla extract

¼ teaspoon salt

Preheat the oven to 350°F (180°C, or gas mark 4). Mix the water and the chia seeds in a large liquid measuring cup and set aside. Place the oats, half of the berries, and half of the walnuts in a 9-inch (23 cm) round baking dish.

Add the nondairy milk, maple syrup, vanilla, and salt to the chia mixture and whisk until well combined. Pour the mixture into the baking dish and gently stir to incorporate. Bake the oatmeal for 45 minutes, until slightly golden in color. The oatmeal should be a little soft, as it will firm slightly while cooling. Let the oatmeal cool on a rack for 20 minutes. Cut it into fifths, place in 5 storage containers, and top each serving with the remaining berries and walnuts. Oatmeal can be stored in the refrigerator for up to 7 days or in the freezer for up to 3 months.

YIELD: 5 SERVINGS

NUTRITIONAL ANALYSIS
Per Serving: 399 calories; 15 g fat; 60 g carbohydrates; 9 g fiber; 23 g sugar; 9 g protein

Tip!
In a pinch, frozen berries work well here. They may get a little soggy in the topping, but they'll still taste good.

FAJITA PITA POCKETS

• FRESH OUTTA THE FRIDGE • 30 MINUTES OR LESS
• UNDER 10 INGREDIENTS • GLUTEN-FREE OPTION • SOY FREE
• NUT FREE • NO SUGAR ADDED

While these fajita pitas would be great as burritos or wraps, I love the ease of shoving all of the delicious fillings into a pita pocket. This recipe comes together so quickly, you could make it on your lunch break!

1 tablespoon (15 ml) organic sunflower oil

2 red bell peppers, sliced into strips

2 green bell peppers, sliced into strips

1 cup (120 g) halved and sliced red onion

¼ teaspoon salt

2 (15-ounce [425 g]) cans vegan refried beans

1 teaspoon garlic powder

1 teaspoon ground cumin

5 pitas or gluten-free wraps if desired

5 cups (205 g) chopped romaine

1 avocado, sliced

5 lime wedges

In a large skillet, heat the oil over medium-high heat. Add the bell peppers and onion and cook until they have some brown edges but are not limp, 5 to 7 minutes. Season with salt to taste. While the peppers and onions are cooking, combine the refried beans, garlic powder, and cumin in a small skillet over medium-low heat and cook until they are warmed through. Set aside.

Toast or warm up the pitas to make them more pliable, if desired, then cut each of them in half. Spread the refried bean mixture onto one inner side of each pita half. Next, divide the pepper-onion mixture, romaine, and sliced avocado evenly among the pitas. Refrigerate the pita pockets, with a lime wedge on the side, in storage containers or bags for up to 7 days. If you prefer to eat them warm, keep the romaine and avocado on the side as you reheat the pocket.

YIELD: 5 SERVINGS

NUTRITIONAL ANALYSIS
Per Serving: 490 calories; 13 g fat; 80 g carbohydrates; 19 g fiber; 8 g sugar; 19 g protein

CREAMY AVOCADO TAHINI ZOODLES

• FRESH OUTTA THE FRIDGE • 30 MINUTES OR LESS • UNDER 10 INGREDIENTS
• GLUTEN-FREE • SOY FREE • NUT FREE • OIL FREE • NO SUGAR ADDED

There's a gluten-free pasta dish on my blog with a sauce that's similar to this one, but in my quest for something more summer friendly, I came up with an updated version that—dare I say it—is even better! The rich, creamy sauce is balanced out by the refreshing zoodles, and the briny olives and bright tomatoes make it a well-rounded meal.

FOR THE ZOODLES:
3 pounds (1.4 kg) zucchini, spiralized
½ teaspoon salt

FOR THE SAUCE:
1 cup (235 ml) full-fat coconut milk
1 cup (215 g) mashed avocado
¼ cup (12 g) chopped chives, divided
¼ cup (15 g) fresh parsley leaves
¼ cup (60 g) tahini
¼ cup (60 ml) lemon juice
¾ teaspoon salt
⅛ teaspoon black pepper

FOR THE ASSEMBLY:
2 (15-ounce [425 g]) cans chickpeas, drained and rinsed
1¼ cups (225 g) chopped tomatoes
½ cup (50 g) halved Kalamata olives

To make the zoodles: Place the spiralized zucchini in a large colander and sprinkle it with the salt, tossing to evenly coat. Set the colander over a bowl and allow the water to drain from the zoodles for 15 to 20 minutes.

To make the sauce: In a food processor equipped with an S-blade, puree the coconut milk, the avocado, 2 tablespoons (6 g) of the chives, the parsley, the tahini, the lemon juice, the salt, and the pepper until very smooth. Season with additional salt to taste.

To assemble: Pat the drained zoodles lightly with a towel and divide them between 5 storage containers. Top them with the avocado-tahini sauce, followed by the chickpeas, tomatoes, olives, and the remaining chives. Chill for 15 to 20 minutes before serving, or store in the refrigerator for up to 6 days.

YIELD: 5 SERVINGS

NUTRITIONAL ANALYSIS
Per Serving: 432 calories; 24 g fat; 45 g carbohydrates; 16 g fiber; 9 g sugar; 16 g protein

Tip!
If you do not have a spiralizer, use a julienne peeler to make zoodles or a regular vegetable peeler to create zucchini "ribbons." Or skip all of that and check your local grocer's produce section for ready-made zoodles.

See the Snack Attack! chapter for the Buckwheat Ginger Balls (page 141), the snack listed in this weekly menu.

Part 3

MIX AND MATCH
FOR ALL

Chapter 1

MIX AND MATCH MENUS

MEAL PLANS FOR FAMILIES, COUPLES, OR MAYBE JUST VEGGIE-ENTHUSIAST ROOMMATES!

If you're not alone in your meal prepping and planning aspirations, this section is for you. Here, I'll break down some suggested five-day meal plans for two or four people, with notes on how to optimize your ingredient prep to save you time and effort during the week!

MENU 1: PUDDING, PEANUT BUTTER, POLENTA PIZZA, OH MY!

• INTERMEDIATE • FOR TWO PEOPLE • GLUTEN-FREE OPTION • SOY-FREE OPTION

A solid mix of sweet and savory dishes that includes tasty handhelds, protein-dense penne Bolognese, and allergy-friendly options for two people. And you definitely don't want to miss these snacks!

	DAY 1	DAY 2	DAY 3	DAY 4	DAY 5
BREAKFAST	Matcha Oatmeal (page 71)	Blood Orange Freezer Waffles with Berry Compote (page 119)	Avocado Lime Pudding Parfaits (page 73)	Matcha Oatmeal (page 71)	Blood Orange Freezer Waffles with Berry Compote (page 119)
LUNCH	Crunchy Lavash Wraps (page 83)	Dill-Roasted Chickpeas with Potato Wedges (page 129)	Crunchy Lavash Wraps (page 83)	Springtime Sheet Pan Polenta Pizza (page 120)	Penne Bolognese (page 113)
DINNER	Dill-Roasted Chickpeas with Wedges (page 129)	Springtime Sheet Pan Polenta Pizza (page 120)	Nacho Potato Bake (page 97)	Penne Bolognese (page 113)	Nacho Potato Bake (page 97)
SNACKS	Pizza Kale Chips (page 152)	Chocolate Peanut Butter Rice Bars (page 153)	Pizza Kale Chips (page 152)	Chocolate Peanut Butter Rice Bars (page 153)	Chocolate Peanut Butter Rice Bars (page 153)

MENU NOTES

There are many components to this menu that can be made ahead of time and aren't too labor intensive. Let's call prep day, when you're getting ready for your week ahead, "Day Zero." This is when you'll prep bulk ingredients and sauces and complete the easier recipes, in this case, breakfasts and wraps.

DAY ZERO CHECKLIST
Equipment
✔ Mixing bowls
✔ High-speed blender and/or food processor
✔ 2 large pots with lids
✔ 2 small pots with lids
✔ Large nonstick skillet
✔ 2 large baking sheets
✔ Cooling rack
✔ 8 x 8-inch (20 x 20 cm) baking dish
✔ 9 x 13-inch (23 x 33 cm) casserole dish
✔ Waffle maker (not Belgian)
✔ Parchment paper
✔ Storage containers and jars

You'll be making:
✔ 1½ batches Lentil Walnut Sausage Crumbles (page 160)
✔ 2 batches Pizza Sauce (page 157)
✔ White Bean Garlic Spread (page 162)
✔ Kimchi Cheese Sauce (page 158)
✔ Sunflower Sour Cream (page 166)
✔ Chocolate Peanut Butter Rice Bars (page 153)
✔ Pizza Kale Chips (page 152)
✔ Matcha Oatmeal (page 71)
✔ ½ batch Avocado Lime Pudding Parfaits (page 73)
✔ Blood Orange Freezer Waffles with Berry Compote (page 119)
✔ Crunchy Lavash Wraps (page 83)

Day Zero Steps
It will help you immensely if you have all of your ingredients laid out and prepped before you start. I like to group all of the ingredients by recipe on my counter so that I don't have to search for anything while I'm prepping.

Step 1: Start by cooking the lentils for the Lentil Walnut Sausage Crumbles. While they're cooking, prepare the Pizza Sauce and set it aside to cool before storing in a container. With the remaining lentil cooking time, make the White Bean Garlic Spread in the food processor, transfer to a bowl, and set aside. Clean out your food processor and pots.

Step 2: Finish the Lentil Walnut Sausage Crumbles and allow them to cool before transferring to a container and refrigerating. Clean your food processor and nonstick pan.

Step 3: Start boiling the cashews and carrots for the Kimchi Cheese Sauce in a large pot and start cooking the sunflower seeds for the Sunflower Sour Cream in a small pot. When they're done, drain them both and set them aside. Meanwhile, make the Chocolate Peanut Butter Rice Bars. Wash the pots.

Step 4: Finish the Kimchi Cheese Sauce, transfer to a storage container, and refrigerate. Clean your blender and finish the Sunflower Sour Cream, and transfer that to a storage container and refrigerate it, too. Wash the blender.

Step 5: Start the Pizza Kale Chips. While the chips are baking, make the Matcha Oatmeal in a large pot, then transfer it to four storage containers and refrigerate. Wash the pot. When the Pizza Kale Chips are done baking, move them to a cooling rack to dry them out further before storing them in a sealed container in a dark, cool place.

Step 6: Prepare a half batch of the Avocado Lime Pudding mixture in the food processor, then layer into two jars with mix-ins; refrigerate. Next, make the waffle batter in your blender and set it aside to thicken while you make the berry compote in a small pot and preheat your waffle iron. While the berries are simmering, start making your waffles.

Step 7: As the waffles finish cooking, move them to a cooling rack. Let the berry compote cool before transferring it to a storage container and refrigerating it. While the waffles are cooking, assemble the Crunchy Lavash Wraps (using the White Bean Garlic Spread you set aside earlier), wrap them in foil or paper, and refrigerate. When the waffles are cool, transfer them to a storage container or zip-top bag and freeze.

Step 8: The rest of the recipes will be prepared throughout the week, with no more than one on each day: You'll make the Dill-Roasted Chickpeas with Potato Wedges on Day 1 and have leftovers for Day 2. You'll make the Springtime Sheet Pan Polenta Pizza on Day 2 and finish it on Day 4. Make the Nacho Potato Bake on Day 3 and have leftovers on Day 5, and make the Penne Bolognese on Day 4 and finish it Day 5.

MENU 2: HIGH-PROTEIN MEALS FOR TWO

• BEGINNER • FOR TWO PEOPLE • GLUTEN-FREE

Super-satiating, protein-rich, and oh-so-flavorful! This menu is for those of you looking to up your plant-based protein intake in the most delicious way possible.

	DAY 1	DAY 2	DAY 3	DAY 4	DAY 5
BREAKFAST	Protein Smoothie Bowl (page 108)	Hash Brown–Crusted Frittata (page 76)	Piña Colada Chia Pudding (page 107)	Protein Smoothie Bowl (page 108)	Hash Brown–Crusted Frittata (page 76)
LUNCH	Chipotle Tempeh Kale Bowls (page 111)	Citrus Lentil Quinoa Salad (page 117)	Chipotle Tempeh Kale Bowls (page 111)	Almond Butter Tofu Stew (page 112)	Citrus Lentil Quinoa Salad (page 117)
DINNER	Seitan Fusion Tacos (page 115)	Almond Butter Tofu Stew (page 112)	Pinto Pecan Lettuce Boats (page 114)	Seitan Fusion Tacos (page 115)	Pinto Pecan Lettuce Boats (page 114)
SNACKS	White Bean Garlic Spread (page 162)	Spinach-Onion Sour Cream Dip (page 146)	Grain-Free Granola (page 149)	Spinach-Onion Sour Cream Dip (page 146)	Grain-Free Granola (page 149)

MENU NOTES

When I first started working on this book, I asked my readers and social media followers what problems they had with meal prepping. So many people said that they longed for some high or higher-protein vegan meal plans, especially people with really active lifestyles! So, here's a work week's worth of higher-protein dishes to keep you satiated.

DAY ZERO CHECKLIST
Equipment

✔ 9-inch (23 cm) cast-iron or other ovensafe skillet
✔ Large sauté pan with lid
✔ 2 large pots with lids
✔ Small pot with lid
✔ Large baking sheet
✔ Blender and/or food processer
✔ Mixing bowls
✔ Storage containers and jars

You'll be making:

✔ Hash Brown–Crusted Frittata (page 76)
✔ Seitan Cutlets (page 168), if not doing the gluten-free option
✔ Gochujang Aioli (page 161)
✔ White Bean Garlic Spread (page 162)
✔ 1¼ batches Sunflower Sour Cream (page 166)
✔ Spinach-Onion Sour Cream Dip (page 146)
✔ Grain-Free Granola (page 149)
✔ Protein Smoothie Bowls (page 108)
✔ Citrus Vinaigrette (page 159)
✔ Citrus Lentil Quinoa Salad (page 117)
✔ Chipotle Tempeh Kale Bowls (page 111)
✔ ½ batch Piña Colada Chia Pudding (page 107)

Day Zero Steps

I've organized the items on this list so that while one thing is baking or simmering, you can get started on something easier, like a blender sauce.

Step 1: Start the Hash Brown-Crusted Frittata. While the frittata is baking, start the Seitan Cutlets. Once the seitan is in the simmering broth, prepare and store the Gochujang Aioli, then make the White Bean Garlic Spread, reserving ½ cup (123 g) for the Chipotle Tempeh Kale Bowls and refrigerating the rest.

Step 2: Take the frittata out of the oven and let it cool on a rack before transferring to storage containers and refrigerating. Transfer the seitan from the simmering broth to a storage container and refrigerate. Wash the pans, food processor, and the blender.

Step 3: Make the Sunflower Sour Cream, then remove ¼ cup (58 g) and store it in the fridge. Use the rest to make the Spinach-Onion Sour Cream Dip. Cut up and refrigerate carrot sticks and celery stalks to eat with the sour cream dip and the white bean dip. Start making the Grain-Free Granola, and, while it's baking, make the stovetop crumble for the Protein Smoothie Bowls and set it aside. Wash the blender and the food processor.

Step 4: After the granola has baked, let it cool to room temperature on a rack, then transfer to a storage container. Assemble the smoothie base and the toppings for the Protein Smoothie Bowls, transfer to storage containers, and freeze.

Step 5: Make the Citrus Vinaigrette and let it chill while starting on the quinoa and lentils for the Citrus Lentil Quinoa Salad. In a separate pot, start the quinoa with kale for the Chipotle Tempeh Quinoa Kale Bowls.

Step 6: While the lentils and quinoa are cooking, prepare the tempeh for the Chipotle Tempeh Kale Bowls. Once everything is cooked, complete and store the Citrus Lentil Quinoa Salad and Chipotle Tempeh Kale Bowls.

Step 7: For an easy finish, make a half-batch of the Piña Colada Chia Pudding and refrigerate. You'll make the Seitan Fusion Tacos on Day 1, the Almond Butter Tofu Stew on Day 2, and the Pinto Pecan Lettuce Boats on Day 3.

MENU 3: MEALS FOR A FAMILY

• BEGINNER • FOR FOUR PEOPLE • GLUTEN-FREE OPTION

Feeding a family can be hard! So many different diets to accommodate, and really, so much cooking. This menu breaks it down to make your life a little easier.

	DAY 1	DAY 2	DAY 3	DAY 4	DAY 5
BREAKFAST	Savory Pastry Pockets (page 75)	Instant Pot Rice Pudding (page 78)	Chocolate Raspberry Smoothie Jars (page 72)	Savory Pastry Pockets (page 75)	Instant Pot Rice Pudding (page 78)
LUNCH	Grilled Gazpacho Verde (page 84)	Classic Tofu Salad Sandwiches (page 92)	Corn Fritter Salad (page 88)	Classic Tofu Salad Sandwiches (page 92)	Corn Fritter Salad (page 88)
DINNER	Hearty Spinach Lasagna (page 123)	Sesame Miso Stir-Fry (page 105)	Hearty Spinach Lasagna (page 123)	Instant Pot Barley Beet Borscht (page 128)	Sesame Miso Stir-Fry (page 105)
SNACKS	Cinnamon Toast Popcorn (page 143)	White Bean Garlic Spread (page 162)	Cinnamon Toast Popcorn (page 143)	White Bean Garlic Spread (page 162)	Chocolate Tahini Nice Cream (page 142)

MENU NOTES

To make sure that this menu wouldn't consume your whole life, I picked recipes that were very easy to double, or already have 8 servings—ahem, lasagna. A lot of this can be made ahead, and while there are still some recipes that require day-of action, they come together easily thanks to your Day Zero prep. As always, if you start out with your prepped ingredients organized by recipe, it will be tremendously helpful.

DAY ZERO CHECKLIST
Equipment

✔ Multicooker or pressure cooker
✔ 2 large pots with lids
✔ Small pot with lid
✔ Large sauté pan
✔ Large skillet
✔ Grill or grill pan
✔ Mixing bowls
✔ 2 large baking sheets
✔ Blender and/or food processer
✔ Heavy objects (like books or large cans) for pressing tofu
✔ Storage containers and jars

You'll be making:

✔ 2 batches Classic Tofu Salad Sandwiches (page 92)
✔ Tofu ricotta and tomato sauce for Hearty Spinach Lasagna (page 123)
✔ 2 batches Savory Pastry Pockets (page 75)
✔ 2 batches Instant Pot Rice Pudding (page 78)
✔ 2 batches Lentil Walnut Sausage Crumbles (page 160)
✔ Chocolate Raspberry Smoothie Jars (page 72)
✔ White Bean Garlic Spread (page 162)
✔ 2 batches Corn Fritter Salad (page 88)
✔ Cashew Ranch (page 167) or Sunflower Sour Cream (page 166)
✔ Grilled Gazpacho Verde (page 84)
✔ Cinnamon Toast Popcorn (page 143)

Day Zero Steps

This list may look intimidating, but I promise we'll get through it together. Your food processor will be your absolute best friend for this menu!

Step 1: Press the tofu for a double batch of Classic Tofu Salad Sandwiches and the tofu ricotta for the Hearty Spinach Lasagna. Take out the frozen spinach for the Savory Pastry Pockets and allow it to thaw. Start a double batch of the Instant Pot Rice Pudding. While the rice is cooking, start the lentils for your double batch of Lentil Walnut Sausage Crumbles.

Step 2: While the lentils are cooking, make the tofu salad, transfer to a storage container, and refrigerate. I recommend storing the tofu salad on its own and toasting the bread for the sandwiches just before serving.

Step 3: Assemble and freeze the Chocolate Raspberry Smoothie Jars, then finish off the rice pudding, divide it and the toppings between 8 storage containers, and refrigerate. Once the lentils are cooked, divide them

in half and finish the crumbles using the food processor and a sauté pan, working in two batches to avoid overcrowding. Preheat the oven for the Savory Pastry Pockets and wash the pot and the food processor.

Step 4: Using one batch of the crumbles, assemble a double batch of the Savory Pastry Pockets. Place them on two large baking sheets and bake, making sure to switch the positions of the baking sheets halfway through.

Step 5: While the pastry pockets are baking, make the White Bean Spread in the food processor and store it in the refrigerator. Then, chop up 3 bell peppers, 4 carrots, and 6 stalks of celery to use as dippers for the bean spread throughout the week. Clean out the food processor and make the Tofu Ricotta, then transfer it to a large storage container and refrigerate.

Step 6: Start the tomato sauce for the lasagna; while it's simmering, make the batter for the corn fritters and set aside. When the tomato sauce is done, let it cool slightly, then transfer it to a storage container and refrigerate.

Step 7: Make the Cashew Ranch or Sunflower Sour Cream, then make the double batch of Corn Fritter Salad. Once those are assembled, refrigerate them, then make and store the Grilled Gazpacho Verde. Finally, make the Cinnamon Toast Popcorn and divide it into 8 small bags or containers. The rest of the recipes are easily made day-of, and now you have all of your components ready for the lasagna!

MENU 4: THE EXPEDIENT MENU

• BEGINNER • FOR TWO PEOPLE • GLUTEN-FREE OPTION

So many of these recipes are either naturally easy and quick to make or they're made in a multicooker to save you even more time!

	DAY 1	DAY 2	DAY 3	DAY 4	DAY 5
BREAKFAST	Breakfast Burritos (page 79)	Mushroom Omelet (page 81)	Buckwheat Breakfast Bowls (page 74)	Breakfast Burritos (page 79)	Mushroom Omelet (page 81)
LUNCH	Grilled Barbecue Cauliflower Bowls (page 89)	Spicy Jackfruit Salad (page 87)	Grilled Barbecue Cauliflower Bowls (page 89)	Spicy Jackfruit Salad (page 87)	Instant Pot Barbecue Soy Curl Sandwiches (page 122)
DINNER	Instant Pot Spaghetti Squash with Pistachio Sage Sauce (page 131)	Cauliflower Chowder (page 99)	Instant Pot Spaghetti Squash with Pistachio Sage Sauce (page 131)	Instant Pot Barley Beet Borscht (page 128)	Cauliflower Chowder (page 99)
SNACKS	Buckwheat Ginger Balls (page 141)	Apples with Tahini Caramel (page 154)	Buckwheat Ginger Balls (page 141)	Apples with Tahini Caramel (page 154)	Buckwheat Ginger Balls (page 141)

MENU NOTES

Because a few of these recipes are made in a multicooker, it takes the pressure off of Day Zero a little bit. You can choose to either get a lot of this done in the one day or just wait until the evening of to make your dinners, which will come together in no time at all.

DAY ZERO CHECKLIST
Equipment
✔ Small pot with lid
✔ Large pot with lid
✔ Large sauté pan
✔ Large skillet
✔ 9-inch (23 cm) skillet
✔ Grill or grill pan
✔ Food processor and/or blender
✔ Mixing bowls
✔ Storage containers and jars

You'll be making:
✔ 1 batch Cilantro Jalapeño Cashew Dressing (page 161)
✔ 1 batch Veggie Barbecue Sauce (page 164)
✔ Buckwheat Ginger Balls (page 141)
✔ Mushroom Omelet (page 81)
✔ Breakfast Burritos (page 79)
✔ Spicy Jackfruit Salad (page 87)
✔ ½ batch Buckwheat Breakfast Bowls (page 74)
✔ Apples with Tahini Caramel (page 154)
✔ Grilled Barbecue Cauliflower Bowls (page 89)

Day Zero Steps
We're going to start with some of the dressings, sauces, and a snack, then get into the main entrees that have more active cooking time. The multicooker recipes are left off this list; they're easy enough to make on the first day you're eating them.

Step 1: Make the Cilantro Jalapeño Cashew Dressing in the blender, then transfer it to a jar or container and refrigerate. Start cooking the carrots for the Veggie Barbecue Sauce. While they're cooking, clean out the blender, then finish the Veggie Barbecue Sauce and set it aside.

Step 2: Make and store the Buckwheat Ginger Balls. Clean out the food processor and make the base for the Mushroom Omelet. Finish the omelet and refrigerate it in storage containers.

Step 3: Next, make and store the Breakfast Burritos. Clean your skillet and make the Spicy Jackfruit Salads. Store the salads in containers and refrigerate.

Step 4: Start cooking the buckwheat for the half batch of Buckwheat Breakfast Bowls. While the buckwheat is cooking, make the Tahini Caramel for the apple slice snack. Finish and store the Buckwheat Breakfast Bowls.

Step 5: Finally, make the Grilled Barbecue Cauliflower Bowls using half of the Veggie Barbecue Sauce; store the other half of the sauce to use in the Instant Pot Barbecue Soy Curl Sandwiches later in the week. As mentioned, the other recipes come together quite quickly and can be made day-of!

MENU 5: LIGHTER FARE

• BEGINNER • FOR TWO PEOPLE

When summer hits, your diet typically changes a bit. Comforting (but heavy) soups, stews, and casseroles just aren't in the picture. Here are a few light dishes for you to enjoy in the warmer months so that you can feel refreshed and energized by your meals.

	DAY 1	DAY 2	DAY 3	DAY 4	DAY 5
BREAKFAST	Chocolate Raspberry Smoothie Jars (page 72)	Shakshuka (page 98)	Peanut Butter Pancake Sandwiches (page 80)	Shakshuka (page 98)	Chocolate Raspberry Smoothie Jars (page 72)
LUNCH	Farro Brussels Spring Salad (page 86)	Cajun Chickpea Salad Wraps (page 93)	Farro Brussels Spring Salad (page 86)	Smoky Tofu Squash Salad (page 130)	Cajun Chickpea Salad Wraps (page 93)
DINNER	Instant Pot Bouillabaisse (page 125)	Smoky Tofu Squash Salad (page 103)	Grilled Chimichurri Seitan Salad (page 101)	Instant Pot Bouillabaisse (page 125)	Grilled Chimichurri Seitan Salad (page 101)
SNACKS	Snacky Seed Clusters (page 105)	Peppery Seitan Jerky (page 148)	Snacky Seed Clusters (page 105)	Peppery Seitan Jerky (page 148)	Snacky Seed Clusters (page 105)

MENU NOTES

Because these are meals are light, you may need to nibble a little more often, so I've included some of my favorite filling snacks. If these meals end up being a little too light, try adding cooked chickpeas, tempeh, or tofu for a boost of protein. Or you could always snack some more, which is my favorite thing to do!

DAY ZERO CHECKLIST
Equipment

✔ Large pot with lid
✔ Small pot with lid
✔ Large sauté pan with lid
✔ Grill or grill pan
✔ Cooling rack
✔ Food processor and/or blender
✔ 2 large baking sheets
✔ Parchment paper
✔ Mixing bowls

You'll be making:

✔ Seitan Cutlets (page 168)
✔ Chimichurri (page 163)
✔ Citrus Vinaigrette (page 159)
✔ Cajun Chickpea Salad Wrap (page 93)
✔ Snacky Seed Clusters (page 105)
✔ Shakshuka (page 98)
✔ Chocolate Raspberry Smoothie Jars (page 72)
✔ Cashew Ranch (page 167)
✔ Farro Brussels Spring Salad (page 86)
✔ Smoky Tofu Squash Salad (page 130)
✔ ½ batch Peanut Butter Pancake Sandwiches (page 80)
✔ Peppery Seitan Jerky (page 148)

Day Zero Steps

While nothing on this menu is too hard to make, Day Zero will get you solidly prepped for the week. We'll start with a few multipurpose basics and dressings that need to chill, then we'll jump into the entrees, going back and forth between getting something going in the oven or on the stove, then fitting in easier recipes during the cooking time.

Step 1: Start the Seitan Cutlets. While they are simmering, prepare the Chimichurri in a food processer, then refrigerate. Make the Citrus Vinaigrette and refrigerate that as well. Wash the food processor.

Step 2: Blend the sauce for the Cajun Chickpea Salad Wraps and set it aside. Remove the seitan from the water and set it aside to cool a bit. Finish the Cajun Chickpea Salad, transfer to a large container, and refrigerate. Wash the blender.

Step 3: Preheat the oven for the Snacky Seed Clusters, then transfer the seitan to a storage container and refrigerate. Prepare the seed clusters and get them into the oven. While they are baking, prepare the shakshuka on the stove. Once the shakshuka is simmering, assemble and freeze the Chocolate Raspberry Smoothie Jars.

Step 4: Transfer the seed clusters to a rack to cool and raise the oven temperature to 400°F (200°C, or gas mark 6) for the Smoky Tofu Squash Salad and then wash the baking sheet. Make and store the cashew ranch. Store the finished shakshuka in the fridge.

Step 5: Start cooking the farro for the Farro Brussels Spring Salad. While that is cooking, prepare the tofu and squash for the Smoky Tofu Squash Salad. Once the sheet pan is in the oven, make the pancake batter for the Peanut Butter Pancake Sandwiches. Heat a large skillet and prepare the pancakes, then set them aside to cool.

Step 6: Once the squash and tofu are done, set the baking sheet on a rack to cool to room temperature. Adjust the oven to 300°F (150°C, or gas mark 2), and line another baking sheet with parchment paper. Start the Seitan Jerky, storing the remaining seitan in the fridge for the Grilled Chimichurri Seitan Salad later in the week. While the seitan is in the oven, finish making the chickpea salad wraps, farro salad, and the tofu squash salad, storing all of them in the refrigerator.

Step 7: Store the cooled seed clusters and jerky. Now, you have most of your dishes made for the week, and you can easily make the last two day- or evening-of.

MENU 6: FLAVORS OF EAST ASIA AND THEN SOME

• BEGINNER • FOR TWO PEOPLE • GLUTEN-FREE OPTION

Some of my favorite dishes come from East Asian cuisines, so naturally I was very inspired by those original dishes for this menu! Make this meal plan and you'll be in for the bold flavors of toasted sesame, kimchi, gochujang, teriyaki, and more.

	DAY 1	DAY 2	DAY 3	DAY 4	DAY 5
BREAKFAST	Mushroom Omelet (page 81)	Matcha Oatmeal (page 71)	Mushroom Omelet (page 81)	Buckwheat Breakfast Bowls (page 74)	Matcha Oatmeal (page 71)
LUNCH	Teriyaki Portobello Edamame Bowls (page 95)	Mushroom Hand Rolls (Temaki) (page 90)	Kimchi Mac and Cheese (page 96)	Teriyaki Portobello Edamame Bowls (page 95)	Mushroom Hand Rolls (Temaki) (page 90)
DINNER	One-Pot Dashi Soba (page 104)	Kimchi Mac and Cheese (page 96)	Teriyaki Tofu with Cauliflower Fried Rice (page 116)	One-Pot Dashi Soba (page 104)	Teriyaki Tofu with Cauliflower Fried Rice (page 116)
SNACKS	Brownie Dip (page 151)	Yogurt Pops (page 142)	Brownie Dip (page 151)	Yogurt Pops (page 142)	Yogurt Pops (page 142)

MENU NOTES

Once you start making these recipes, you'll see that a lot of the ingredients are repeated, which makes grocery shopping (and prepping) a little easier. Also, there are five recipes with mushrooms of different kinds on this menu, so if you're a mushroom hater, beware!

DAY ZERO CHECKLIST

Equipment

✔ Large sauté pan
✔ Large skillet
✔ Small pot
✔ 2 large pots with lids
✔ Multicooker (optional) or a large pot with lid
✔ Food processor and/or blender
✔ 9-inch (23 cm) skillet
✔ Popsicle molds
✔ Mixing bowls

You'll be making:

✔ Teriyaki Portobello Edamame Bowls (page 95)
✔ Mushroom Hand Rolls (page 90)
✔ Kimchi Cheese Sauce (page 158)
✔ ½ batch Ginger Teriyaki Sauce (page 156)
✔ Brownie Dip (page 151)
✔ ½ batch Buckwheat Breakfast Bowls (page 74)
✔ Yogurt Pops (page 142)
✔ Matcha Oatmeal (page 71)
✔ Mushroom Omelet (page 81)

Day Zero Steps

Your Day Zero is about to be filled with a lot of veggie prep, so get ready to practice your knife skills. Other than that, a lot of these recipes come together easily, and will set you up nicely for finishing your other recipes during the week.

Step 1: Start the rice for the Teriyaki Portobello Edamame Bowls and the Mushroom Hand Rolls. If you're using a multicooker, combine 3⅓ cups (785 ml) water, 2⅔ cups (505 g) short grain brown rice, 2 tablespoons (30 ml) rice vinegar, and a pinch of salt in the multicooker and bring to high pressure, cook for 19 minutes, let sit for 5 minutes, then quick-release the rest of the pressure. If you're cooking your rice on the stove, combine 5⅓ cups (1.3 L) water with the rice, vinegar, and salt amounts above in a large pot, bring to a boil, then adjust the heat to medium-low and simmer, with vented lid, for 30 to 35 minutes, or until the rice is tender.

Step 2: While the rice is cooking, start cooking the cashews and carrots for the Kimchi Cheese Sauce, then start the half batch of Ginger Teriyaki Sauce. Finish and store both sauces in the fridge. Once the rice is done, let it cool uncovered (in whatever vessel you used) while you prepare and store the Brownie Dip and whatever dippers you want to serve it with. Wash the food processor and the pots.

Step 3: Start cooking the buckwheat for a half batch of the Buckwheat Breakfast Bowls, and while it's cooking, assemble and freeze the yogurt pops. Finish and store the buckwheat bowls, then make and store the Matcha Oatmeal.

Step 4: Now that the rice has cooled considerably, assemble and store the Mushroom Hand Rolls. Start cooking the mushrooms for the Teriyaki Portobello Edamame Bowls, and divide the rest of the bowl ingredients between 4 storage containers. When the mushrooms are done, add them to the containers, then refrigerate.

Step 5: Lastly, make and store the Mushroom Omelets. Now you have a solid start on the week!

MENU 7: LUNCH AND DINNER FOR TWO (PLUS OPTIONS FOR KIDS)

• BEGINNER • FOR TWO PEOPLE • GLUTEN-FREE OPTION

Sometimes you need the freedom of flying by the seat of your pants for one meal slot a week! This lunch and dinner menu gives you the flexibility of choosing whatever you want for breakfast, whether that's your favorite smoothie or something from the coffee shop you always go to before work. If you have kids, there are some easy recipes here to make meal time more efficient.

	DAY 1	DAY 2	DAY 3	DAY 4	DAY 5
LUNCH	Mushroom Hand Rolls (Temaki) (page 90)	Tropical Cucumber Chili Salad (page 85)	Mushroom Hand Rolls (Temaki) (page 90)	Tropical Cucumber Chili Salad (page 85)	Instant Pot Creamy Broccoli Soup (page 126)
DINNER	Instant Pot Creamy Broccoli Soup (page 126)	Mushroom Onion Burgers (page 103)	Brussels Carrot Quiche (page 109)	Mushroom Onion Burgers (page 103)	Brussels Carrot Quiche (page 109)
KIDS OPTIONS	Veggie Bento Boxes (page 133)	Kidney Bean Sliders with Sweet Potato Fries (page 136)	Veggie Bento Boxes (page 133)	Kidney Bean Sliders with Sweet Potato Fries (page 136)	Veggie Quesadillas (page 135)

MENU NOTES

Because the breakfast dishes would normally be made on Day Zero, our prep is going to be way easier for this menu! There are also notes on how to prep some kid options if you need them. For more snacks and kid-friendly foods, see Chapter 7 (page 132).

DAY ZERO CHECKLIST
Equipment
✔ Large sauté pan
✔ Large pot
✔ Multicooker or another large pot with lid
✔ Food processor and/or blender
✔ 2 large baking sheets
✔ Parchment paper
✔ Spiralizer or julienne peeler
✔ Pie crust/pan
✔ Mixing bowls

You'll be making:
✔ Mushroom Hand Rolls (Temaki) (page 90)
✔ Veggie Bento Boxes (page 133)
✔ Mushroom Onion Burgers (page 103)
✔ Kidney Bean Sliders with Sweet Potato Fries (page 136)
✔ Tropical Cucumber Chili Salad (page 85)
✔ Instant Pot Creamy Broccoli Soup (page 126)

Day Zero Steps
Honestly, this menu is nearly easy enough to make everything the first day you're eating it, but these few simple steps will help save some extra time throughout the week.

Step 1: Start the rice for the Mushroom Hand Rolls and the Veggie Bento Boxes. If you're using a multicooker, combine 2¾ cups (650 ml) water, 2¼ cups (428 g) short grain brown rice, 2 tablespoons (30 ml) rice vinegar, and a pinch of salt in the multicooker and bring to high pressure, cook for 19 minutes, let sit for 5 minutes, then quick-release the rest of the pressure. If you're cooking your rice on the stove, combine 4½ cups (1.1 L) water with the rice, vinegar, and salt amounts above in a large pot, bring to a boil, then adjust the heat to medium-low and simmer, with vented lid for 30 to 35 minutes or until the rice is tender.

Step 2: While the rice is cooking, preheat the oven to 375°F (190°C, or gas mark 5) and prepare the Mushroom Onion Burger patties and the Kidney Bean Slider patties by making 1½ batches of the Mushroom Onion Burger patty recipe. Place the four large patties on one baking sheet and the four small patties on another baking sheet. Prep the fries for the sliders and put them on the sheet with the small patties. Bake the burgers and fries.

Step 3: While the burgers are baking, start the mushroom onion burger topping. While that cooks assemble the Tropical Cucumber Chili Salad and refrigerate, storing the seasoning separately. Once the burgers and topping are complete, refrigerate them.

Step 4: Once the rice is done, allow it to cool while you clean out the multicooker and make the Instant Pot Creamy Broccoli Soup. While the soup is cooling, prepare the mushroom filling for the hand rolls.

Step 5: Once the rice is done, allow it to cool while you clean out the multicooker and make the Instant Pot Creamy Broccoli Soup. While the soup is cooling, prepare the mushroom filling for the hand rolls.

Chapter 2

BEAUTIFUL BREAKFASTS

HERE ARE SEVERAL GREAT REASONS WHY YOU SHOULDN'T SKIP MY FAVORITE MEAL OF THE DAY!

I'm one of those people that would rather prep the night before and then sleep longer in the morning. Because of this, it was important to me that there be plenty of make-ahead or made-in-minutes breakfast options for you in this chapter.

MATCHA OATMEAL

- *NEEDS SOME HEAT* • *30 MINUTES OR LESS*
- *UNDER 10 INGREDIENTS* • *GLUTEN-FREE*
- *SOY FREE* • *NUT FREE*

Oatmeal has always been a favorite breakfast of mine because it is so easy to customize and comes together in minutes! Here I've added a little matcha powder for a light caffeine kick and wonderful flavor. The sweetness of the oatmeal goes perfectly with tart raspberries!

3½ cups (830 ml) water

3 cups (323 g) rolled oats

1 cup (235 ml) plain unsweetened nondairy milk,
divided

1/3 cup (80 ml) agave nectar

2 teaspoons (10 ml) vanilla
extract

2 teaspoons (6 g) culinary
matcha powder

1/8 teaspoon salt

1 cup (125 g) fresh
raspberries

¼ cup (20 g) unsweetened
coconut flakes

½ teaspoon black sesame
seeds

In a large pot over medium heat, bring the water, oats, and ¾ cup (175 ml) of the nondairy milk to a boil. Adjust the heat to medium-low and simmer, stirring occasionally, until the oats start to break down and become creamy, 5 to 7 minutes. While the oats are cooking, whisk together the remaining nondairy milk, agave nectar, vanilla, and matcha powder in a small ramekin or bowl until there are no clumps.

Add the matcha mixture and the salt to the oatmeal, stirring until combined. When the oatmeal has thickened to your liking, divide it between 4 bowls or storage containers, then top with raspberries, coconut flakes, and sesame seeds. Serve while warm or store in the refrigerator for up to 7 days.

YIELD: 4 SERVINGS

NUTRITIONAL ANALYSIS
Per serving: 414 calories; 8 g fat; 74 g carbohydrates; 10 g fiber;
25 g sugar; 11 g protein

CHOCOLATE RASPBERRY SMOOTHIE JARS

• *FREEZER FRIENDLY* • *30 MINUTES OR LESS* • *UNDER 10 INGREDIENTS*
• *GLUTEN FREE* • *SOY FREE* • *NUT FREE* • *OIL FREE*

Some days I'm craving a bright, tropical smoothie to start my day, but other times, I need something a little richer and this chocolate raspberry number hits the spot! The little bit of caffeine from the cocoa probably doesn't hurt, either.

3 cups (545 g) frozen raspberries

2 cups (390 g) chopped bananas

1 cup (67 g) firmly packed chopped kale, stems removed

½ cup (70 g) hemp hearts

¼ cup (20 g) cocoa powder

¼ cup (38 g) coconut sugar

Pinch salt

4 cups (960 ml) water

Set out 4 24-ounce (710 ml) wide mouth jars. Layer ¾ cup (135 g) frozen raspberries, ½ cup (97 g) bananas, and ¼ cup (17 g) kale into each jar. Next, divide the hemp hearts, cocoa powder, coconut sugar, and salt evenly among the jars; screw the lids on and store in the freezer.

When you're ready to make a smoothie, run warm water over the outside of one jar to help release the items inside. Pour the jar's contents into a blender, followed by 1 cup (235 ml) water. Blend until completely smooth, then transfer back to the jar and serve.

YIELD: 4 SERVINGS

NUTRITIONAL ANALYSIS
Per serving: 269 calories; 4 g fat;
56 g carbohydrates; 12 g fiber;
32 g sugar; 11 g protein

Tip!
I love to add a half scoop of my favorite vegan chocolate protein powder to these smoothie jars to give them even richer chocolate flavor!

AVOCADO LIME PUDDING PARFAITS

• FRESH OUTTA THE FRIDGE • 30 MINUTES OR LESS • UNDER 10 INGREDIENTS • GLUTEN-FREE • SOY FREE • NUT FREE • OIL FREE

While avocado is good on damn near everything, it's especially versatile in sweet recipes. You've probably seen it used as a sneaky ingredient in chocolate pudding, but I love showing off its green color and brightening its flavor with lime in this breakfast parfait.

2 cups (440 g) mashed
    avocado
¾ cup (175 ml) plain
    unsweetened nondairy
    milk
1/3 cup (80 ml) agave nectar
3 tablespoons (45 ml) lime
    juice and 2 teaspoons
    (4 g) zest
Pinch salt
2 cups (290 g) fresh
    blueberries
½ cup (70 g) raw pumpkin
    seeds (pepitas)

In a food processor equipped with an S-blade, process the avocado, nondairy milk, agave nectar, lime juice and zest, and salt until completely smooth, scraping down the sides as needed.

Set out 4 jars or storage containers with lids. To layer the parfaits, scoop about 1/3 cup (80 g) pudding into each jar, followed by ¼ cup (38 g) blueberries and 1 tablespoon (10 g) pumpkin seeds. Repeat for a second set of layers, then refrigerate the parfaits until chilled. Parfaits can be stored in the refrigerator for up to 5 days.

YIELD: 4 SERVINGS

NUTRITIONAL ANALYSIS
Per serving: 412 calories; 25 g fat; 48 g carbohydrates; 11 g fiber;
30 g sugar; 9 g protein

While chilling the pudding allows the flavors to really meld together for optimum results, if you're short on time, you can keep all of your ingredients in the refrigerator before assembling and forgo the chill time!

BUCKWHEAT BREAKFAST BOWLS

• NEEDS SOME HEAT • 30 MINUTES OR LESS • UNDER 10 INGREDIENTS
• GLUTEN FREE • SOY FREE • OIL FREE

My love affair with buckwheat began only a few years ago, but I'm still sad that it didn't start earlier! This versatile, gluten-free grain is easy to cook, has a wonderfully nutty flavor, and is excellent in this breakfast bowl.

2 cups (475 ml) water

1⅓ cups (228 g) buckwheat groats

1 cup (235 ml) plain unsweetened nondairy milk

¼ cup (60 ml) maple syrup, plus more for optional drizzling

2 tablespoons (10 g) cocoa powder

2 teaspoons (10 ml) vanilla extract

¼ teaspoon ground cinnamon

⅛ teaspoon salt

3 cups (450 g) sliced bananas

¼ cup (65 g) natural almond butter

Bring the water and buckwheat groats to a boil in a large pot. Adjust the heat to medium-low, cover, and simmer stirring occasionally until the groats are tender, 12 to 15 minutes. Adjust the heat to low and stir in nondairy milk, maple syrup, cocoa powder, vanilla, cinnamon, and salt. Adjust seasoning and consistency as desired (the buckwheat should be of a porridge consistency).

Divide the buckwheat between 4 bowls or storage containers and top with bananas, almond butter, and a little drizzle of maple syrup, if using. Serve warm or store in the refrigerator for up to 7 days.

YIELD: 4 SERVINGS

NUTRITIONAL ANALYSIS
Per serving: 481 calories; 10 g fat; 83 g carbohydrates; 7 g fiber; 27 g sugar; 13 g protein

SAVORY PASTRY POCKETS

• NEEDS SOME HEAT • FREEZER FRIENDLY • NO SUGAR ADDED

My local coffee shop has these vegan fajita pastry pockets that I am absolutely enamored with—and thankful for on particularly busy mornings—so I was inspired to create my own homemade variation! Instead of fajita mix-ins, I went with my savory Lentil Walnut Sausage Crumbles, sun-dried tomatoes, spinach, and vegan cheese (the cheese is optional, but I highly recommend it here)

2 sheets (17.3 ounces, 490 g) vegan puff pastry

½ batch (about 1½ cups [200 g]) Lentil Walnut Sausage Crumbles (page 160)

1 cup (85 g) frozen chopped spinach, thawed

½ cup (58 g) vegan cheese shreds, optional

¼ cup (25 g) diced green onion

2 tablespoons (18 g) minced oil-packed sun-dried tomatoes, plus 1 tablespoon (15 ml) oil

¼ teaspoon coarse salt

1/8 teaspoon black pepper

Preheat the oven to 400°F (200°C, or gas mark 6). Lay out your sheets of puff pastry on their own sheets of parchment, and carefully roll them each into an 8 x 10-inch (20 x 25 cm) rectangle. Combine the Lentil Walnut Sausage Crumbles, spinach, cheese, green onion, and sun-dried tomatoes in a large bowl.

Score light lines into one sheet of puff pastry, marking halfway lengthwise and widthwise to create equal-sized quadrants. Place ½ cup (100 g) of the filling in each quadrant, patting it into a firm rectangle and leaving a border of at least ½ inch (1 cm) around it for sealing. Using your finger or a pastry brush, wet the borders of each quadrant with a little water, then carefully lay the second sheet of pastry on top.

Cut the quadrants apart using a knife or a pizza cutter, then secure the edges of the pastry by pressing them with a fork. Using the fork, poke a couple of holes into the top of each pastry for ventilation. Transfer the parchment paper with the pastry pockets to a baking sheet. Brush the sun-dried tomato oil over the tops of the pockets, then sprinkle each pocket with salt and black pepper. Bake until the edges start to brown, about 25 minutes.

Serve warm or let cool on a rack until they reach room temperature before storing in a sealed container in the refrigerator for up to 7 days or in the freezer for up to 3 months. Reheat in a toaster or toaster oven.

YIELD: 4 PASTRIES

NUTRITIONAL ANALYSIS
Per serving: 724 calories; 47 g fat; 64 g carbohydrates; 8 g fiber; 5 g sugar; 16 g protein

Tip!
If this sounds delicious but you don't eat gluten, I recommend loading up a gluten-free tortilla with this filling and heating it on a hot skillet or panini press.

Not feeling the cheese shreds? Try subbing in 1/2 cup (120 g) White Bean Garlic Spread (page 162)!

HASH BROWN–CRUSTED FRITTATA

• NEEDS SOME HEAT • FREEZER FRIENDLY • GLUTEN FREE • SOY FREE • NUT FREE • NO SUGAR ADDED

Tip!
I love adding ½ cup (56 g) of vegan cheddar shreds to the top of the frittata before baking for an extra layer of flavor.

While I do love a good omelet, sometimes I get a little anxious about the flipping. Frittatas are great because all you have to do is cook your favorite fillings in a pan, add your base, and leave it to the oven to take care of the rest. This breakfast frittata is rich in protein, easy to make, and delicious atop a bed of mixed greens.

1 tablespoon (15 ml) sun-flower oil, divided

8 ounces (225 g) frozen shredded potato hash browns

⅛ teaspoon salt

¼ teaspoon black pepper, divided

2 cups (260 g) sliced bell peppers, assorted colors

1 cup (110 g) sliced yellow onion

1 cup (135 g) chickpea flour

⅓ cup (30 g) nutritional yeast

2 tablespoons (16 g) cornstarch

2 teaspoons *Kala namak* (Indian black salt; see note on page 169)

1 teaspoon onion powder

½ teaspoon baking powder

¼ teaspoon ground turmeric, optional

14 ounces (425 ml) hot vegetable broth

1 (15-ounce [425 g]) can black beans, drained and rinsed

In a 9-inch (23 cm) cast iron skillet or oven-safe pan, heat 2 teaspoons of the oil over medium heat. Add the hash browns, pressing gently to flatten them into an even layer. Cook until there is some browning on the first side, about 6 minutes, sprinkling the salt and ⅛ teaspoon pepper over the top while they are cooking. Carefully flip the patty onto a plate and set aside. Preheat the oven to 375°F (190°C, or gas mark 5).

Add the remaining 1 teaspoon oil to the skillet along with the bell peppers and onion, and cook, stirring occasionally, until the onions are nearly translucent, about 5 minutes, then remove from the pan and set aside. While the peppers and onions are cooking, whisk together the chickpea flour, nutritional yeast, cornstarch, kala namak, onion powder, baking powder, and turmeric, if using, in a large bowl. Pour the hot vegetable broth into the chickpea flour mixture and whisk until combined.

Slide the hash brown patty, uncooked side down, back into the skillet, then top with black beans and pepper-onion mixture. Whisk the chickpea mixture to recombine (don't worry about how thin it is) and pour it over the top. Place the skillet in the oven and bake for 33 to 35 minutes, or until the top is matte and slightly firm.

Remove the skillet from the oven and let cool on a rack for 15 to 20 minutes before serving. If storing for later, wait 30 minutes before cutting the frittata into quarters. Transfer to 4 storage containers and store in the refrigerator for up to 7 days or in the freezer for up to 3 months (allow to defrost completely in the refrigerator before reheating).

YIELD: 4 SERVINGS

NUTRITIONAL ANALYSIS
Per serving: 370 calories; 6 g fat; 60 g carbohydrates; 16 g fiber; 5 g sugar; 19 g protein

Note: If you don't have an ovensafe skillet or pan, brown the hash browns on the stovetop as instructed, then transfer them to a pie dish or springform pan before assembling.

INSTANT POT RICE PUDDING

- *NEEDS SOME HEAT* - *FREEZER FRIENDLY* - *30 MINUTES OR LESS*
- *UNDER 10 INGREDIENTS* - *GLUTEN FREE* - *SOY FREE*
- *NUT FREE* - *OIL FREE*

Oats have a special place in my heart, but this brown rice pudding is a welcome change of pace—and it comes together so easily in an Instant Pot! Comforting but not over-the-top heavy, this pudding is made even better with fresh fruits and little cacao nibs.

1¾ cups (415 ml) water

1½ cups (285 g) short grain brown rice

2 cinnamon sticks

1 teaspoon vanilla extract

1 orange

1 (13.5-ounce [400 ml]) can light coconut milk

¼ cup (60 ml) maple syrup

2 cups (340 g) sliced strawberries

2 cups (290 g) blackberries

4 teaspoons (15 g) cacao nibs

Combine the water, rice, cinnamon sticks, and vanilla in an Instant Pot or pressure cooker. Slice the peel off of the orange in large pieces and add the strips to the pot. Secure the lid and bring the pot to high pressure, then cook for 20 minutes. Turn off the heat and let sit for 10 minutes before quick-releasing the remaining pressure. While the rice is cooking, chop the orange into small pieces, taking care to remove any seeds, and set aside.

Discard the orange peels and cinnamon sticks, then stir in the coconut milk and maple syrup. Simmer over low heat for 5 minutes. Divide the pudding between 4 bowls or storage containers, then top with reserved oranges, strawberries, blackberries, and cacao nibs. The pudding can be stored in the refrigerator for up to 7 days or in the freezer for up to 2 months.

YIELD: 4 SERVINGS

NUTRITIONAL ANALYSIS
Per serving: 433 calories; 10 g fat; 88 g carbohydrates; 11 g fiber; 26 g sugar; 6 g protein

Tip!
To save money, keep frozen berries in your freezer all year long. They're perfect for recipes like this, where it's not imperative to use fresh berries.

BREAKFAST BURRITOS

• *NEEDS SOME HEAT* • *FREEZER FRIENDLY* • *30 MINUTES OR LESS*
• *GLUTEN-FREE OPTION* • *NUT FREE* • *NO SUGAR ADDED*

I could eat breakfast burritos pretty much every day of my life. Now, with this easy, filling, and delicious recipe, I am well on my way, and you can be, too! These babies are freezer-friendly, so feel free to double the batch and store some in your freezer for mornings when you just don't feel like cooking.

FOR THE HASH BROWNS:
3 tablespoons (45 ml) sunflower oil
16 ounces (455 g) frozen shredded potato hash browns
¼ teaspoon salt
⅛ teaspoon black pepper

FOR THE SCRAMBLE:
2 teaspoons sunflower oil
1 cup (140 g) diced yellow onion
1 (14-ounce [397 g]) package firm tofu, drained
3 tablespoons (25 g) Vegan Eggy Seasoning (page 169)

FOR THE ASSEMBLY:
4 burrito-size tortillas or 8 gluten-free wraps
3 cups (120 g) firmly packed chopped kale
1 cup (210 g) salsa
½ cup (58 g) vegan cheese shreds (optional)

To make the hash browns: Heat the oil in a large skillet over medium heat. Add the hash browns, pressing gently to flatten them into an even layer. Cook for 6 minutes on one side, then flip (you can do this in pieces) and cook for another 6 to 8 minutes or until they are getting golden brown.

To make the scramble: While the hash browns are cooking, heat the oil in a sauté pan over medium heat. Add the onion and cook until translucent, about 5 minutes. Crumble in the tofu and cook until the water has mostly evaporated, about 5 minutes. Stir in the Vegan Eggy Seasoning and cook for another 2 minutes.

To assemble: Warm the tortillas in the microwave or one at a time over a gas stove burner until pliable. Divide the hash browns evenly among the centers of the tortillas, then top with tofu scramble, kale, salsa, and cheese, if using. Working with one burrito at a time, wrap up the tortilla by folding two sides of the tortilla towards the center, then rolling the unfolded end closest to you over the filling. Keep rolling until the wrap is completely closed. Serve while warm or store in the refrigerator in a lunch container or wrapped in foil for up to 5 days or in the freezer for up to 3 months.

YIELD: 4 SERVINGS

NUTRITIONAL ANALYSIS
Per serving: 501 calories; 15 g fat; 65 g carbohydrates; 10 g fiber; 5 g sugar; 24 g protein

PEANUT BUTTER PANCAKE SANDWICHES

• NEEDS SOME HEAT • FREEZER FRIENDLY
• 30 MINUTES OR LESS • SOY FREE

Not to toot my own horn, but whenever my dude and I host family or friends overnight, I make these pancakes in the morning for a guaranteed hit. Vegan or not, pancakes are the bridge that can unite us all. To make them a little more travel-friendly, I've opted for a sandwich form, filled with nut butter and fresh fruit!

1 cup (235 ml) plain unsweet-
    ened nondairy milk
2 teaspoons (10 ml) apple
    cider vinegar
1 cup (125 g) unbleached
    all-purpose flour
½ cup (63 g) whole wheat
    pastry flour
1 teaspoon ground cinnamon
1 teaspoon baking powder
½ teaspoon baking soda
½ teaspoon salt
2 tablespoons (30 ml) water
2 tablespoons (20 g) sugar
1 tablespoon (15 ml) olive
    oil, plus extra for greasing
    the pan
1½ teaspoons (8 ml) vanilla
    extract
½ cup (130 g) natural
    smooth peanut butter
2 cups (340 g) sliced
    strawberries

In a large liquid measuring cup, combine the nondairy milk and vinegar and set aside. In a bowl, sift together the all-purpose flour, pastry flour, cinnamon, baking powder, baking soda, and salt. Whisk the water, sugar, olive oil, and vanilla into the nondairy milk mixture until sugar dissolves, then pour it into the flour mixture. Whisk until there are no dry pockets but there are still some small lumps left in the batter.

Heat a large skillet or griddle over medium-low heat and brush it with a thin layer of oil. Using a ¼ cup (60 ml) measure, portion batter onto the skillet, spreading out each pancake until it is roughly 4 inches (10 cm) across. Cook until first sides are golden-brown, 2 to 3 minutes, then flip and cook until second sides are golden-brown, another 1 to 2 minutes. Transfer pancakes to a plate and repeat with the remaining batter; you should have 8 pancakes.

If eating right away, spread one side of 4 of the pancakes with peanut butter, top with strawberry slices, and place other 4 pancakes on top to make sandwiches. If storing for later, let the pancakes cool completely before transferring them to a storage container and storing them in the refrigerator for up to 7 days or in the freezer for up to 3 months. Store the peanut butter and strawberries separately.

YIELD: 4 SERVINGS

NUTRITIONAL ANALYSIS
Per serving: 438 calories; 20 g fat; 53 g carbohydrates; 7 g fiber;
11 g sugar; 13 g protein

MUSHROOM OMELET

• NEEDS SOME HEAT • 30 MINUTES OR LESS
• GLUTEN FREE • NUT FREE • NO SUGAR ADDED

While there are a few very solid vegan egg products on the market nowadays, I still think homemade is best! I've tinkered with different omelet recipes over the years, and I really think this one is awesome. The combination of silken tofu with chickpea flour gives this protein-rich breakfast an excellent texture, and you don't have to wait very long for it to cook

12 ounces (340 g) silken tofu

1 cup (235 ml) vegetable broth

¾ cup (94 g) chickpea flour

3 tablespoons (25 g) Vegan Eggy Seasoning (page 169)

1 tablespoon (8 g) cornstarch

1 teaspoon baking powder

Cooking spray

Salt

Black pepper

8 ounces (225 g) sliced cremini mushrooms

2 cups (40 g) loosely packed spinach, arugula, or mixed greens

¼ cup (30 g) halved and sliced red onion

Puree the tofu, vegetable broth, chickpea flour, Vegan Eggy Seasoning, cornstarch, and baking powder in a blender or food processor equipped with an S-blade until completely smooth; set aside.

Heat a 9-inch (23 cm) skillet over medium heat and spray lightly with cooking spray. Pour ¾ cup (175 ml) of the tofu mixture into the pan, tilting the pan so the bottom is completely covered. Cook until the edges start to turn golden-brown, 3 to 4 minutes. Carefully flip the omelet, sprinkle it with salt and black pepper, then top it with one-quarter of the mushrooms, greens, and onions. Cook until the bottom is golden-brown, 3 to 4 minutes, then flip half of the omelet over onto itself and slide onto a plate. Repeat with the remaining tofu mixture and vegetables.

Serve the omelets immediately or allow them to cool to temperature before transferring to storage containers and storing in the refrigerator for up to 7 days.

YIELD: 4 SERVINGS

NUTRITIONAL ANALYSIS
Per serving: 209 calories; 6 g fat;
31 g carbohydrates; 6 g fiber;
6 g sugar; 21 g protein

Note: This recipe is light, although the protein content is high. If you want to bulk it up, add some vegan cheese shreds to the filling and/or serve the omelets with a side of hash browns or fresh fruit.

Chapter 3

BUNCHES OF LUNCHES

NO FROZEN MEALS HERE! YOU'LL BE LOOKING FORWARD TO THESE DISHES ALL MORNING LONG.

Your coworkers and fellow students are about to be wowed by your lunches! And not in a seafood-in-the-lunchroom kind of way. These recipes are so good, you may need to make a double batch to share—or not.

CRUNCHY LAVASH WRAPS

• FRESH OUTTA THE FRIDGE • 30 MINUTES OR LESS
• GLUTEN-FREE OPTION • SOY FREE • NUT FREE • OIL FREE

These wraps are my version of K.I.S.S. when it comes to lunchtime. They're easily made in under 30 minutes, even including the homemade sauce! Fresh veggies and seeds give a nice crunch to these handheld, delicious wraps. If you're not familiar with lavash, think of it as the love child of a flatbread and a tortilla. You can now find it in most markets!

4 lavash wraps or gluten-free tortillas
1 recipe White Bean Garlic Spread (page 162)
½ cup (73 g) toasted sunflower seeds
½ cup (50 g) diced green onion
2 red bell peppers, stemmed, seeded, and sliced into strips
3 carrots, julienned
4 ounces (115 g) fresh spinach
1 avocado, sliced thin

Lay out the four wraps and spread about ⅓ cup (80 g) of the White Bean Garlic Spread on each one. Top the spread with green onion, sunflower seeds, bell peppers, carrots, spinach, and avocado, leaving a 2-inch (5 cm) border at one end to act as a seam.

Starting from the short side opposite the "seam," carefully roll up each wrap. Serve or wrap in sandwich paper or foil and store in the refrigerator for up to 5 days.

YIELD: 4 SERVINGS

NUTRITIONAL ANALYSIS
Per serving: 458 calories; 23 g fat; 50 g carbohydrates; 15 g fiber; 9 g sugar; 18 g protein

GRILLED GAZPACHO VERDE

**• FRESH OUTTA THE FRIDGE • 30 MINUTES OR LESS
• GLUTEN FREE • SOY FREE • OIL FREE • NO SUGAR ADDED**

I've made plenty of tomato-based gazpachos, which are an excellent way to use up that summer garden bounty. However, this green version is definitely my new favorite, because of its added grilled flavor and refreshing toppings!

FOR THE GAZPACHO:
3 poblano or Anaheim peppers
1 jalapeño
1 pound (455 g) tomatillos with husks removed
1 red onion, sliced in half
1 cup (235 ml) water
1 cup (120 g) corn kernels
½ cup (68 g) raw cashews
¼ cup (8 g) loosely packed cilantro
2 tablespoons (30 ml) lime juice
1 clove garlic
Salt

FOR THE TOPPING:
1½ cups (205 g) diced cucumbers
1 cup (120 g) corn kernels
1 cup (135 g) diced avocado
2 tablespoons (5 g) minced cilantro
1 tablespoon (15 ml) lime juice
¼ teaspoon salt
⅛ teaspoon black pepper

To make the gazpacho: Using a grill or grill pan, carefully char the poblanos and jalapeño until the skins are nearly black, then place them in a bowl and cover it so the peppers can steam. Grill the tomatillos and red onion until they have softened slightly and have bold, visible grill marks. Uncover the bowl and carefully scrape the charred skin from the peppers using a butter knife. Stem and seed the peppers and transfer them to a large blender pitcher.

Cut the tomatillos into quarters and cut the red onion pieces in half, then add them to the blender along with the water, corn, and cashews. Blend until the mixture is very smooth, then let it settle for 5 minutes before adding the cilantro, lime juice, and garlic and blending again until very smooth. (If your blender is on the smaller side, you may need to do this in batches.) Season with salt to taste, then divide the gazpacho between 4 bowls or storage containers and refrigerate while you assemble the topping.

To make the topping: Combine the cucumbers, corn, avocado, cilantro, lime juice, salt, and pepper in a small bowl. Once the gazpacho is thoroughly chilled, top each serving with some of the salsa. The topped gazpacho can be stored in the refrigerator for up to 5 days.

YIELD: 4 SERVINGS

NUTRITIONAL ANALYSIS
Per serving: 301 calories; 14 g fat; 38 g carbohydrates; 11 g fiber; 14 g sugar; 8 g protein

TROPICAL CUCUMBER CHILI SALAD

• FRESH OUTTA THE FRIDGE • 30 MINUTES OR LESS • UNDER 10 INGREDIENTS • GLUTEN FREE • SOY FREE • OIL FREE • NO SUGAR ADDED

In Southern California, you'd be hard pressed to miss the fruit carts on so many street corners. On a hot summer day, they're heaven sent and topping their fruit cups with Tajín makes them even better. This salad was inspired by those flavors.

1½ pounds (680 g) cucumbers, spiralized
1½ cups (233 g) diced pineapple
1 cup (175 g) diced mango
½ cup (50 g) halved and thinly sliced red onion
½ cup (8 g) loosely packed chopped cilantro
2 tablespoons (30 ml) lime juice
1 cup (137 g) roasted cashews
1 tablespoon (8 g) chili powder
½ teaspoon salt
Pinch cayenne pepper

In a large bowl, combine spiralized cucumber, pineapple, mango, onion, cilantro, and lime juice. Divide between 4 bowls or storage containers and top with roasted cashews. In a small bowl or ramekin, combine the chili powder, salt, and cayenne. Sprinkle salad with chili seasoning just before serving. Unseasoned salad can be stored in the refrigerator for up to 7 days.

YIELD: 4 SERVINGS

NUTRITIONAL ANALYSIS
Per serving: 311 calories; 19 g fat; 34 g carbohydrates; 5 g fiber; 18 g sugar; 8 g protein

Tip!
If you do not have a spiralizer, you can make cucumber noodles with a julienne peeler or a standard vegetable peeler.

FARRO BRUSSELS SPRING SALAD

• FRESH OUTTA THE FRIDGE • UNDER 10 INGREDIENTS
• GLUTEN-FREE OPTION • SOY FREE

This salad is the perfect way to move from winter to spring. Brussels and citrus are winter staples, but can grow until mid-spring, while berries are the definitive marker of warmer weather's arrival. All of these flavors play off of each other for a simple, delicious lunch offering.

2 cups (475 ml) water
1 cup (180 g) farro
¼ teaspoon salt
5 cups (400 g) shaved
    Brussels sprouts
1 cup (140 g) sliced
    strawberries
1 batch Citrus Vinaigrette
    (page 159)
1 cup (137 g) roasted salted
    cashews

Combine water, farro, and salt in a covered pot and bring to a boil. Adjust the heat to medium-low and simmer until the grains are soft and the water has been soaked up, about 25 minutes. (Use this time to prep the Brussels sprouts.) Spread the farro out on a baking sheet to cool; you can expedite cooling by placing the sheet in the refrigerator.

In a large bowl, combine the cooled farro, Brussels sprouts, and strawberries. Add half of the Citrus Vinaigrette and toss to coat. Divide between 4 bowls or storage containers and top with cashews. Serve with the remaining dressing or store undressed salad in the refrigerator for up to 5 days.

YIELD: 4 SERVINGS

NUTRITIONAL ANALYSIS
Per serving: 482 calories; 21 g fat; 61 g carbohydrates; 9 g fiber;
12 g sugar; 16 g protein

Tip!
If you don't eat wheat, try replacing the farro with tricolor quinoa.

SPICY JACKFRUIT SALAD

• FRESH OUTTA THE FRIDGE • 30 MINUTES OR LESS
• GLUTEN FREE • SOY FREE

It was funny to read feedback from my testers on this recipe. Almost all of them were slightly terrified at the idea of eating jackfruit cold because of their experiences with store-bought marinated jackfruit. But all of their worries subsided when they took a bite of this salad—it's booming with flavor, and is a textural masterpiece!

FOR THE JACKFRUIT:

2 teaspoons (10 ml) sunflower oil
1 (20-ounce [565 g]) can young jackfruit in brine, drained, seeded, and shredded
3 tablespoons (45 ml) water
1 tablespoon (15 ml) lime juice
1 chipotle pepper in adobo, minced, plus 1 tablespoon (15 ml) adobo sauce
2 teaspoons ground cumin
1 teaspoon agave nectar
½ teaspoon chili powder
½ teaspoon salt

FOR THE SALAD:

8 cups (360 g) chopped lettuce
1 cup (120 g) corn kernels
1 cup (140 g) roasted pumpkin seeds (pepitas)
½ cup (70 g) diced red onion
1 batch Cilantro Jalapeño Cashew Dressing

To make the jackfruit: Heat the oil in a large sauté pan over medium heat. Press any excess moisture out of the jackfruit with paper towels, then add the jackfruit to the pan and cook, stirring occasionally, until the edges begin to brown, 7 to 10 minutes. In a small bowl, whisk together the water, lime juice, chipotle pepper and adobo sauce, cumin, agave nectar, chili powder, and salt. Pour the mixture over the jackfruit and cook for 3 more minutes, then remove the pan from the heat and set aside.

To make the salad: Divide the lettuce between 4 bowls or storage containers then top with the jackfruit, corn kernels, pumpkin seeds, and onion. Serve with dressing, or store undressed salads and dressing separately in the refrigerator for up to 7 days.

YIELD: 4 SERVINGS

NUTRITIONAL ANALYSIS
Per serving: 483 calories; 27 g fat; 49 g carbohydrates; 12 g fiber; 19 g sugar; 19 g protein

Tip!
While you can find canned jackfruit in more stores now, I prefer buying the large cans from international markets. I've found Aroy-D has the best quality jackfruit.

CORN FRITTER SALAD

• FRESH OUTTA THE FRIDGE • 30 MINUTES OR LESS
• GLUTEN-FREE OPTION • SOY FREE • NUT-FREE OPTION

This unique salad may not be everyday fare, but I know you'll love this combination! The corn fritters are like veggie-filled cornbread: fluffy and savory, with a little crispness and subtle sweetness. To balance them out, I've paired the fritters with a light and refreshing salad, a cool dressing, and a hint of lemon.

FOR THE FRITTERS:

1½ cups (210 g) corn meal

¼ cup (31 g) unbleached all-purpose flour, gluten-free if desired

2 tablespoons (20 g) sugar

1 tablespoon (5 g) nutritional yeast

2 teaspoons (9 g) baking powder

1 teaspoon onion powder

1 teaspoon salt

1 cup (235 ml) plain unsweetened nondairy milk

1½ cups (175 g) corn kernels

¼ cup (35 g) diced yellow onion

2 tablespoons (9 g) minced jalapeño

¼ cup (60 ml) sunflower oil, divided

FOR THE SALAD:

8 cups (240 g) firmly packed mixed greens

2 cups (360 g) diced tomatoes

2 cups (320 g) diced cucumbers

4 lemon wedges

½ cup (120 ml) Cashew Ranch (page 167) or Sunflower Sour Cream (page 166)

To make the fritters: In a large bowl, whisk together corn meal, flour, sugar, nutritional yeast, baking powder, onion powder, and salt until combined. Add the nondairy milk and stir until there are no dry pockets. Fold in corn kernels, onion, and jalapeño.

In a large skillet, heat 2 tablespoons (30 ml) of the oil over medium heat. Using a ⅓ cup (80 ml) measure portion the batter onto the skillet and flatten slightly. Cook for 2 minutes, then flip and cook an additional 2 minutes. Transfer the fritters to a paper towel–lined plate and repeat with the remaining oil and batter; you should have 8 fritters.

To make the salad: Divide the greens between 4 plates or storage containers and top with the tomatoes, cucumbers, and lemon wedges. Top each salad with 2 fritters and serve with dressing, or store undressed salads and dressing separately in the refrigerator for up to 7 days. Just before serving, reheat the fritters in a toaster, toaster oven, or microwave, then add them back to the salad and drizzle with dressing.

YIELD: 4 SERVINGS

NUTRITIONAL ANALYSIS
Per serving: 459 calories;
19 g fat; 65 g carbohydrates;
8 g fiber; 13 g sugar;
8 g protein

Tip!
If topping this salad with the Sunflower Sour Cream, thin it out with 2 tablespoons (30 ml) water before drizzling it over the salad.

GRILLED BARBECUE CAULIFLOWER BOWLS

• NEEDS SOME HEAT • 30 MINUTES OR LESS
• GLUTEN FREE • SOY FREE • NUT FREE

Make this bowl during the summer and you won't regret it! Cooking inside when it's hot out can be downright awful, so set that quinoa up on the stove and then move the rest of your cooking to the grill to keep your kitchen, and you, from overheating.

FOR THE QUINOA:

2 cups (475 ml) vegetable broth
1 cup (173 g) quinoa, rinsed

FOR THE BOWLS:

1 medium head (about 24 ounces [680 g]) cauliflower, stemmed and cut into florets
1 cup (240 g) Veggie Barbecue Sauce, divided
Salt
Black pepper
Oil for grill
8 ounces (225 g) green beans, ends trimmed
2 ears corn

Tip!
If you don't have a grill or a grill pan, try using a panini press to "grill" the veggies in batches.

To make the quinoa: Combine the broth and quinoa in a large pot. Cover, bring to a boil, then adjust the heat to medium-low and simmer until the liquid has been absorbed and the grains are soft, 15 to 17 minutes. Remove from the heat, fluff the quinoa with a fork, and cover to keep warm.

To make the bowls: While the quinoa is cooking, heat your grill to 375°F (190°C, or gas mark 5) or heat a grill pan over medium-high heat on the stove. In a large bowl, combine the cauliflower, ½ cup (120 g) of the Veggie Barbecue Sauce, salt, and black pepper, tossing everything together until evenly coated. Brush the grill grate with oil until it is well greased. Grill the florets until they're slightly tender and well browned on all sides, about 15 minutes overall. (I like to grill both sides of the stem, then finish the florets on their heads.)

Transfer the cauliflower back to the bowl, coat with the remaining barbecue sauce, and cover the bowl so that the florets can soften in the steam. Grill the green beans and corn cobs for 5 minutes, flipping them halfway through. Transfer the green beans to another bowl, season with salt and pepper, and cover them so they can steam. Slice the kernels off the cobs (you should have 1 cup [120 g] kernels) and add them to the bowl with the green beans.

Divide the quinoa between 4 bowls or storage containers and top with the cauliflower, green beans, and corn kernels. Serve hot, or store in the refrigerator for up to 7 days.

YIELD: 4 SERVINGS

NUTRITIONAL ANALYSIS
Per serving: 244 calories; 13 g fat; 41 g carbohydrates; 7 g fiber; 14 g sugar; 8 g protein

MUSHROOM HAND ROLLS (TEMAKI)

• FRESH OUTTA THE FRIDGE • GLUTEN FREE • SOY-FREE OPTION • NUT FREE

I always think of hand rolls as fun, edible, and delicious food bouquets. The hand-held aspect of temaki makes them great for eating on the go, but they also make great sushi bowls when deconstructed. Either way, you'll love this recipe!

FOR THE RICE:

1½ cups (355 ml) water or 2½ cups (590 ml) if cooking rice on stove

1¼ cups (238 g) short grain brown rice

1 tablespoon (15 ml) unseasoned rice vinegar

Pinch salt

FOR THE FILLING:

2 teaspoons (10 ml) toasted sesame oil

6 ounces (170 g) shiitake mushrooms, stemmed and chopped

¼ cup (31 g) diced water chestnuts

2 teaspoons (10 ml) tamari or coconut aminos, plus extra for serving

8 sheets nori, halved lengthwise

2 teaspoons (5 g) toasted sesame seeds

1 avocado, sliced

1 cup (130 g) julienned cucumber, cut into 2-inch (5 cm) lengths

½ cup (62 g) julienned carrot, cut into 2-inch (5 cm) lengths

½ cup (58 g) julienned daikon radish, cut into 2-inch (5 cm) lengths

Gochujang Aioli (page 161) for serving, optional

To make the rice in a multicooker: Combine 1½ cups (355 ml) water, rice, rice vinegar, and salt in a multicooker and bring to high pressure, cook for 19 minutes, let sit for 5 minutes, then quick-release the rest of the pressure. Transfer the rice to a bowl and chill in the refrigerator.

To make the rice on the stovetop: Combine 2½ cups (590 ml) water, rice, rice vinegar, and salt in a pot, bring to a boil, then adjust heat to medium-low and simmer, with vented lid, until rice is tender and liquid is absorbed, 30 to 35 minutes. Transfer the rice to a bowl and chill in the refrigerator.

To make the filling: Heat the sesame oil in a sauté pan over medium-high heat. Add the mushrooms, water chestnuts, and tamari to the pan and cook until the mushrooms have softened and any excess liquid has evaporated, about 7 minutes. Set mushroom mixture aside to cool.

Set the nori sheets out on the counter. Working with one half-sheet of nori at a time, place the sheet on the counter with the long edge closest to you. Spread 3 tablespoons (30 g) of the cooked rice evenly over the left half of the sheet. Sprinkle the rice lightly with sesame seeds, then arrange 1 tablespoon (10 g) of the mushroom mixture, a slice of avocado, and a few pieces of cucumber, carrot, and daikon diagonally on top of the rice, so that the vegetables are pointing toward the top left corner of the nori. Starting with the short, left-hand side, roll the nori toward the top right corner, diagonally over the fillings and into a cone shape. When you are almost done rolling, smash a grain of cooked rice onto the bottom right corner and press it onto the cone to seal it. Repeat with remaining 15 half-sheets of nori and remaining vegetables.

Serve with additional tamari and Gochujang Aioli, if using. Hand rolls can be stored in the refrigerator for up to 5 days.

YIELD: 4 SERVINGS

NUTRITIONAL ANALYSIS
Per serving: 355 calories; 12 g fat; 56 g carbohydrates; 11 g fiber; 4 g sugar; 8 g protein

CLASSIC TOFU SALAD SANDWICHES

• FRESH OUTTA THE FRIDGE • 30 MINUTES OR LESS
• GLUTEN-FREE OPTION • NUT FREE • NO SUGAR ADDED

Considering how often I make tofu salad sandwiches, you'd think I would have more printed recipes for them. I finally posted three versions of my favorite lunch to my blog for the first time, and they were such a hit, I knew I had to include one in this book, too! Fair warning: Once you make these, you'll want to repeat them again and again in your meal plans and for summer picnics.

1 (14-ounce [397 g]) package firm tofu, drained

1 (15-ounce [425 g]) can white beans, drained and rinsed

¼ cup (60 g) vegan mayo

1½ tablespoons (23 g) relish

1 tablespoon (11 g) yellow mustard

¼ teaspoon *kala namak* (Indian black salt; see note on page 169)

⅛ teaspoon black pepper

½ cup (60 g) diced celery

¼ cup (35 g) diced red onion

8 slices of toasted bread, gluten-free if desired

⅛ teaspoon smoked paprika, optional

2 cups (40 g) loosely packed mixed greens or lettuce

Press the tofu in a tofu press or by wrapping it in a kitchen towel and setting a flat, heavy object on top of it to press out some of the moisture. Let it sit for 15 minutes, then transfer to a large bowl.

Add the beans, mayo, relish, mustard, kala namak, and black pepper to the bowl and, using a fork or pastry cutter, mash everything together until it resembles a chunky egg salad. Fold in the celery and red onion and adjust seasonings to taste. Next lay out 4 pieces of toasted bread and divide the tofu salad mixture between them. Sprinkle smoked paprika, if using, over the salad, then top with mixed greens, and the remaining pieces of toasted bread.

Serve, or store, wrapped in sandwich paper or in storage containers in the refrigerator for up to 5 days.

YIELD: 4 SANDWICHES

NUTRITIONAL ANALYSIS
Per serving: 391 calories; 12 g fat; 48 g carbohydrates; 10 g fiber; 14 g sugar; 23 g protein

CAJUN CHICKPEA SALAD WRAPS

• FRESH OUTTA THE FRIDGE • 30 MINUTES OR LESS • GLUTEN-FREE OPTION
• SOY FREE • OIL FREE

Cool, creamy, crunchy, and with just the right amount of spice, these Cajun Chickpea Salad Wraps come together in no time at all and are a great lunch for bringing with you to school or work. Honestly, the cashew sauce alone makes this worthwhile—make extra and put it on everything!

2 (15-ounce [425 g]) cans chickpeas, drained, ⅔ cup (160 ml) liquid reserved

¾ cup (90 g) raw cashews

2 tablespoons (10 g) nutritional yeast

1 tablespoon (6 g) Cajun spice blend

1 tablespoon (15 ml) white vinegar

½ teaspoon agave nectar

½ teaspoon salt

1 cup (150 g) diced red bell pepper

1 cup (120 g) corn kernels

¼ cup (35 g) diced red onion

4 burrito-sized tortillas or 8 gluten-free wraps

8 leaves romaine, cut in half widthwise

Puree the reserved chickpea liquid, cashews, nutritional yeast, Cajun spice, vinegar, agave nectar, and salt in a blender until very smooth. Let sit for 5 minutes, then blend again until very smooth. Meanwhile, combine the chickpeas, bell pepper, corn, and red onion in a large bowl.

Pour the sauce over the chickpea mixture and stir to evenly coat everything. (The sauce may seem thin, but it will thicken as it chills.) Refrigerate the chickpea salad for 15 minutes, then stir well. Warm the tortillas in the microwave or one at a time over a gas stove burner until pliable. Place 4 pieces of romaine in the center of each tortilla and top with chickpea salad.

Working with one tortilla at a time, wrap up the tortilla by folding two sides of the tortilla toward the center, then rolling the unfolded end closest to you over the filling. Keep rolling until the wrap is completely closed. Serve right away, or store in the refrigerator in a lunch container or wrapped in foil for up to 5 days.

YIELD: 4 SERVINGS

NUTRITIONAL ANALYSIS
Per serving: 563 calories; 17 g fat; 80 g carbohydrates; 15 g fiber; 11 g sugar; 23 g protein

Chapter 4

ARRAY OF ENTREES

LOOKING FOR YOUR MULTIPURPOSE MAINS? THEY'RE RIGHT HERE!

The dishes in this chapter are super versatile, perfect for rounding out any of your weekly meal plans. Eat them for dinner and have the leftovers for lunch—or maybe even breakfast if you're into that kind of chaos.

TERIYAKI PORTOBELLO EDAMAME BOWLS

• NEEDS SOME HEAT • 30 MINUTES OR LESS
• GLUTEN FREE • NUT FREE

While the teriyaki-glazed portobello mushrooms are the star of the show in this simple dish, the edamame, brown rice, and veggies are all tied for best supporting ingredients. Nutrient dense, flavorful, and easy to make, this bowl is what most meals strive to be!

FOR THE RICE:

1⅓ cups (253 g) short grain brown rice

1 tablespoon (15 ml) unseasoned rice vinegar

FOR THE BOWLS:

1 pound (455 g) portobello mushrooms, sliced into ½-inch (1 cm)–thick strips

Pinch salt

1 cup (235 ml) Ginger Teriyaki Sauce (page 156)

2 cups (190 g) shelled cooked edamame

2 cups (170 g) shredded red cabbage

2 cups (120 g) shredded carrots

Looking to use up the rest of your Ginger Teriyaki Sauce? Try making the Teriyaki Tofu with Cauliflower Fried Rice (page 116)!

To make the rice in a multicooker: Combine 1⅔ cups (390 ml) water, rice, and rice vinegar in a multicooker and bring to high pressure, cook for 19 minutes, let sit for 5 minutes, then quick-release the rest of the pressure.

To make the rice on the stovetop: Combine 2⅔ cups (640 ml) water, rice, and rice vinegar in a pot, bring to a boil, then adjust heat to medium-low and simmer, with vented lid, until rice is tender and liquid is absorbed, 30 to 35 minutes.

To make the bowls: While the rice is cooking, heat a large sauté pan over medium-high heat. Add the mushrooms to the pan and sprinkle with salt to draw out some of their liquid and make them easier to cook without oil. If they get stuck, add a little water to the pan. Cook the mushrooms until they are tender and reduced in size, about 10 minutes. Adjust the heat to medium-low and add the Ginger Teriyaki Sauce to the pan, cooking for another 2 to 3 minutes.

Divide the rice, mushrooms, edamame, cabbage, and carrots, between 4 bowls or storage containers. Drizzle any sauce left in the pan over each serving. Serve warm, or store in the refrigerator for up to 7 days.

YIELD: 4 SERVINGS

NUTRITIONAL ANALYSIS
Per serving: 461 calories; 8 g fat; 35 g carbohydrates; 10 g fiber; 25 g sugar; 20 g protein

KIMCHI MAC AND CHEESE

• *NEEDS SOME HEAT* • *30 MINUTES OR LESS*
• *GLUTEN-FREE OPTION*

If you're familiar with me, my blog *Vegan Yack Attack*, or any of my cookbooks, you know that vegan mac is my *thing*. Naturally, I couldn't put out another book without making a fun and flavorful mac for y'all! And I think this one may just be in my top three, which says a lot considering I've made over 25 different vegan macs over the years.

3 cups (405 g) macaroni pasta

2 teaspoons (10 ml) toasted sesame oil

8 ounces (225 g) shiitake mushrooms, sliced

1 tablespoon (15 ml) tamari

2 teaspoons rice vinegar

1 batch Kimchi Cheese Sauce (page 158)

1 cup (200 g) vegan kimchi, drained

¼ cup (65 g) Gochujang Aioli (page 161), (optional)

¼ cup (25 g) chopped green onions

1 teaspoon sesame seeds

Cook pasta according to the package directions, then strain, reserving 1 cup (235 ml) pasta water; set aside. While the macaroni is cooking, heat the sesame oil in a sauté pan over medium heat. Add the mushrooms to the oil and cook for 5 minutes, then add tamari and rice vinegar. Stir to combine and cook for another 2 minutes before removing from the heat.

Rinse out the pasta pot and add the Kimchi Cheese Sauce to it, warming it over medium-low heat until the starch has activated and it thickens slightly. Add the cooked pasta and stir to evenly coat, adding pasta water, 1 tablespoon (15 ml) at a time, if the sauce seems too thick. Season with salt to taste.

Divide mac and cheese between 4 bowls or storage containers, then top with the mushrooms, kimchi, Gochujang Aioli, green onions, and sesame seeds. Serve warm, or store in the refrigerator for up to 7 days.

YIELD: 4 SERVINGS

NUTRITIONAL ANALYSIS
Per serving (with aioli): 430 calories; 16 g fat; 54 g carbohydrates; 6 g fiber; 7 g sugar; 16 g protein

NACHO POTATO BAKE

- • **NEEDS SOME HEAT** • **GLUTEN FREE** • **SOY FREE**
- • **OIL FREE** • **NO SUGAR ADDED**

I feel as though this book is quickly becoming my love letter to potatoes of every variety. They're just so damn good! Switching the usual chips out for chopped potatoes in this Nacho Potato Bake makes for way better meal prepping—not everyone enjoys soggy chips.

2 pounds (907 g) russet potatoes, scrubbed and diced

½ teaspoon salt

2 tablespoons (18 g) diced pickled jalapeños

½ teaspoon ground cumin

½ teaspoon chili powder

1 batch Kimchi Cheese Sauce (page 158)

1 (15-ounce [425 g]) can low-sodium black beans, drained and rinsed

¼ cup (55 g) Sunflower Sour Cream (page 166) or store-bought vegan sour cream

1 cup (150 g) quartered cherry tomatoes

½ avocado, diced

1 radish, halved and sliced thin

1 tablespoon (1 g) chopped cilantro

4 lime wedges

Preheat oven to 400°F (200°C, or gas mark 6). Spread the potatoes in a 9 x 13-inch (23 x 33 cm) baking dish and sprinkle with the salt, tossing to evenly coat. Cover the dish with foil and roast for 30 minutes, until the potatoes are just underdone.

Stir the jalapeños, cumin, and chili powder into the Kimchi Cheese Sauce, then pour it over the potatoes. Bake for another 15 to 20 minutes, until the potatoes are tender. Top with black beans and drizzle on Sunflower Sour Cream. Finish off with tomatoes, avocado, radish, and cilantro. Serve with lime wedges. Nachos can be stored in the refrigerator for up to 5 days.

YIELD: 4 SERVINGS

NUTRITIONAL ANALYSIS
Per serving: 611 calories; 24 g fat; 83 g carbohydrates; 17 g fiber; 8 g sugar; 21 g protein

Did you make a whole batch of Sunflower Sour Cream? Use the rest to make a partial batch of the Spinach-Onion Sour Cream Dip (page 146) or use it on the Pinto Pecan Lettuce Boats (page 114)!

*Tip!
If you are saving this meal for later, I recommend keeping the avocado separate until after reheating.*

SHAKSHUKA

- **NEEDS SOME HEAT** • **30 MINUTES OR LESS**
- **GLUTEN FREE** • **NUT FREE** • **NO SUGAR ADDED**

A few years ago, I had a bounty of tomatoes from my garden. I asked Instagram, "What the heck should I make with these?" So many commenters suggested shakshuka! I finally figured out a cool way to make the poached eggs vegan friendly, so you won't be disappointed with how all of my experimenting turned out!

Note: Though shakshuka is typically served for breakfast, I don't love tomatoey things in the morning, so I've listed it as an entrée for more flexible eating!

FOR THE EGGS:

12 ounces (340 g) firm silken tofu, drained

2 tablespoons (12 g) Vegan Eggy Seasoning (page 169)

1 tablespoon (8 g) cornstarch

2 tablespoons (30 ml) water

1 tablespoon (5 g) nutritional yeast

¼ teaspoon ground turmeric

Salt

FOR THE SHAKSHUKA:

2 teaspoons (10 ml) sunflower oil

1 cup (140 g) diced yellow onion

1 green bell pepper, stemmed, seeded, and diced

¼ cup (45 g) diced roasted red peppers

2 cloves garlic, minced

2 tablespoons (33 g) tomato paste

1 (28-ounce [794 g]) can diced tomatoes

2 teaspoons (5 g) ground cumin

1 teaspoon paprika

⅛ teaspoon cayenne pepper

Salt

Black pepper

2 tablespoons (8 g) chopped flat-leaf parsley

Sliced bread for serving

To make the eggs: Process the tofu, Vegan Eggy Seasoning, and cornstarch in a food processor equipped with an S-blade until completely smooth. Transfer ¼ cup (35 g) of the tofu mixture to a bowl and whisk in the water, nutritional yeast, and turmeric until smooth. Season with salt to taste; this will be your yolk.

To make the shakshuka: Heat the oil in a large skillet over medium heat. Add the onion and green bell pepper and cook until the vegetables have softened, about 5 minutes. Add the red peppers and garlic and cook for 1 minute, then stir in the tomato paste. Add the diced tomatoes, cumin, paprika, and cayenne pepper, adjust the heat to medium-low, and simmer for 5 minutes. Add salt and pepper to taste, then make six wells in the tomato mixture.

Dollop the white tofu mixture into the wells, spreading so that they aren't thick blobs. Cover and simmer over low heat for 15 minutes. Spoon the "yolks" onto the center of each "egg white," cover, and simmer for another 5 minutes. At this point the "egg whites" should be firm but jiggly. Remove from heat, top with parsley, and serve with sliced bread. To store, allow shakshuka to cool for 15 minutes before dividing between 4 storage containers and storing in the refrigerator for up to 7 days.

YIELD: 4 SERVINGS

NUTRITIONAL ANALYSIS

Per serving (without bread): 201 calories; 5 g fat; 27 g carbohydrates; 5 g fiber; 11 g sugar; 13 g protein

CAULIFLOWER CHOWDER

• **NEEDS SOME HEAT** • **FREEZER FRIENDLY** • **GLUTEN-FREE OPTION**
• **SOY FREE** • **NO SUGAR ADDED**

Maybe you've already noticed based on many of the recipes in this cookbook, but I love potatoes. A lot. But even with all of that love, it is nice to switch up classic dishes using another vegetable, as is the case with this Cauliflower Chowder. If you're looking for a hearty soup that isn't too heavy, this is your recipe!

1 tablespoon (15 ml) sunflower oil or vegan butter
1 cup (140 g) diced yellow onion
1 cup (130 g) diced carrot
1 cup (100 g) diced celery
⅓ cup (42 g) unbleached all-purpose flour or gluten-free flour
2½ cups (570 ml) vegetable broth
1 pound (455 g) cauliflower, stemmed and chopped into bite-sized pieces
1 teaspoon garlic powder
½ teaspoon dried parsley
3 bay leaves
Ground white pepper
1½ cups (355 ml) plain unsweetened nondairy milk
¼ cup (34 g) raw cashews
Salt

In a large pot, heat the oil over medium heat. Add the onion, carrot, and celery and cook until the onions are translucent, about 5 minutes. Add the flour and cook for 1 minute, then add the broth, cauliflower, garlic powder, parsley, bay leaves, and a pinch of white pepper. Cover and bring to a boil, then adjust heat to medium-low and simmer for 10 minutes.

Remove and discard the bay leaves, then transfer about 1 cup (100 g) of the cauliflower pieces to a blender. Add the nondairy milk and cashews to the blender and puree until very smooth, then stir the mixture back into the pot. Cover simmer for 5 more minutes, then season with salt to taste. Transfer to 4 bowls or storage containers and serve warm, store in the refrigerator for up to 7 days, or freeze for up to 6 months.

YIELD: 4 SERVINGS

NUTRITIONAL ANALYSIS
Per serving: 183 calories; 7 g fat; 26 g carbohydrates; 6 g fiber; 7 g sugar; 6 g protein

Tip!
I love to enjoy this soup with oyster crackers for the texture and pop of salt that they add.

SAVORY RIS-OAT-O

• NEEDS SOME HEAT • 30 MINUTES OR LESS • GLUTEN FREE
• SOY FREE • NO SUGAR ADDED

Yes, I know, the name is dorky. But I've always been a fan of puns, whether supremely cheesy or very clever. In this case, I'm giving you a savory oat recipe that serves as a risotto, but without the extra time and steps that are needed to get a true risotto just perfect. Rolled oats cut the cooking time by more than half compared to Arborio rice or steel-cut oats, and the veggie topping rounds it out perfectly.

FOR THE RIS-OAT-O:

4 cups (945 ml) vegetable broth
2½ cups (255 g) rolled oats
½ cup (40 g) nutritional yeast
1 teaspoon garlic powder
½ cup (120 ml) plain unsweetened nondairy milk
1 tablespoon (15 ml) white wine vinegar or lemon juice
Salt

FOR THE TOPPING:

2 teaspoons (10 ml) sunflower oil
1 cup (140 g) diced yellow onion
1 pound (455 g) cremini mushrooms, sliced
2 cups (114 g) firmly packed chopped kale, stems removed
½ cup (68 g) pine nuts
¼ cup (40 g) diced sundried tomatoes, drained
Salt
Black pepper

To make the ris-oat-o: In a medium pot, bring the vegetable broth, oats, nutritional yeast, and garlic powder to a boil over medium heat. Adjust the heat to medium-low and simmer for 5 to 7 minutes, stirring occasionally. When the oats have broken down and are creamy, stir in the nondairy milk, vinegar, and salt to taste.

To make the topping: While the oats are cooking, heat the oil in a large sauté pan over medium heat. Add the onions and cook until they're nearly translucent, about 3 minutes. Add the mushrooms to the pan and cook until the mushrooms are soft, have reduced in size, and there is no excess liquid, 5 to 7 minutes.

Adjust the heat to medium-low, add the kale, pine nuts, and sundried tomatoes to the pan, and cook until the kale is wilted and the pine nuts are golden, about 2 minutes. Season with salt and black pepper to taste. Divide the ris-oat-o between 4 bowls or storage containers, then top with mushroom-kale mixture and serve, or store in the refrigerator for up to 7 days.

YIELD: 4 SERVINGS

NUTRITIONAL ANALYSIS
Per serving: 422 calories; 18 g fat; 65 g carbohydrates; 11 g fiber; 10 g sugar; 25 g protein

GRILLED CHIMICHURRI SEITAN SALAD

• FRESH OUTTA THE FRIDGE • SOY FREE • NUT FREE
• NO SUGAR ADDED

Even though this ingredient list is super short, it is powerful! Savory, lean seitan is coated in herby, acidic Chimichurri and then grilled to create a medley of flavors. Creamy avocado, crunchy romaine, and ripe tomatoes lighten this dish up and add a variety of textures to go with the meaty slices of seitan. Oh dear, I've drooled on the keyboard.

16 ounces (455 g) Seitan Cutlets (6 pieces) or store-bought seitan, sliced
1 batch Chimichurri (page 163)
8 cups (320 g) chopped romaine
1½ cups (225 g) diced tomatoes
1 large avocado, diced

Heat a grill or grill pan over medium heat. Brush the seitan with a generous coating of Chimichurri (there will be a fair amount left for drizzling over the salad). Grill the seitan for 10 minutes, flipping halfway through grilling. Transfer to a plate and let cool for 5 minutes.

Meanwhile, divide the romaine, tomatoes, and avocado between 4 bowls or storage containers. Slice the seitan into ½-inch (1 cm) thick strips and divide them evenly among the servings. Drizzle with the remaining Chimichurri and serve, or store in the refrigerator for up to 7 days.

YIELD: 4 SERVINGS

NUTRITIONAL ANALYSIS
Per serving: 432 calories; 24 g fat; 30 g carbohydrates; 6 g fiber; 5 g sugar; 25 g protein

Tip!
To add even more texture to this salad, top it with your favorite croutons or serve with a slice of crusty toasted bread.

MUSHROOM ONION BURGERS

• *NEEDS SOME HEAT* • *FREEZER FRIENDLY* • *GLUTEN-FREE OPTION*
• *SOY-FREE OPTION* • *NUT FREE* • *NO SUGAR ADDED*

You gotta love a good veggie burger! Except for when they're a mushy mess—no thank you. These burgers have great texture and are never mushy, thanks to the mixture of walnuts, oats, beans, and mushrooms. Plus, the sautéed topping just takes it to another level.

½ cup (50 g) raw walnuts

½ cup (45 g) quick-cooking oats

1 teaspoon smoked paprika

1 teaspoon onion powder

1 teaspoon dried parsley

Black pepper

1 large yellow onion, sliced into rings, divided

1 (15-ounce [425 g]) can kidney beans, drained and rinsed

6 ounces (170 g) sliced cremini mushrooms, divided

1 tablespoon (15 ml) olive oil

1 tablespoon (15 ml) tamari or coconut aminos

Salt

1 tablespoon (15 ml) sunflower oil

1 tablespoon (15 ml) red wine or water

4 slices vegan provolone or smoked gouda (optional)

4 burger buns, gluten-free if desired

2 cups (40 g) baby arugula

Preheat the oven to 375°F (190°C, or gas mark 5) and line a baking sheet with parchment paper. Pulse the walnuts, oats, smoked paprika, onion powder, dried parsley, and ¼ teaspoon black pepper in a food processor equipped with an S-blade until the walnuts are fine crumbles. Dice ½ cup (60 g) of the onion rings and add to the processor along with the beans, ½ cup (40 g) of the mushrooms, the olive oil, the tamari, and ½ teaspoon salt. Pulse until it forms a dough, being careful not to overprocess into a paste.

Form the mixture into four patties, roughly 4 inches (10 cm) wide and ½ inch (1 cm) thick. Place them on the prepared baking sheet and bake for 20 minutes, then flip the patties and bake for another 15 minutes.

Meanwhile, heat the sunflower oil in a sauté pan over medium heat. Add the remaining onions and cook until the onions are translucent and beginning brown on the edges, about 7 minutes. Reduce the heat to medium-low, add the remaining mushrooms and a pinch of salt to release their moisture, and cook for 10 minutes, stirring occasionally. Deglaze the pan with the wine and simmer for 2 more minutes. Season with salt and black pepper to taste.

When the burgers are done, top each one with a slice of vegan cheese, if using, and place on bottom buns. Top with the mushroom mixture, arugula, and, lastly, the top buns. Serve immediately or store in the refrigerator for up to 5 days in airtight containers.

YIELD: 4 SERVINGS

NUTRITIONAL ANALYSIS
Per serving: 548 calories; 23 g fat; 75 g carbohydrates; 11 g fiber; 9 g sugar; 22 g protein

Tip!
If you're not eating these right away, prep the patties, bake them for 20 minutes, then take them out of the oven and let them cool to room temperature. Then, store them in an airtight container layered with pieces of wax paper in the freezer for up to 3 months.

ONE-POT DASHI SOBA

• NEEDS SOME HEAT • 30 MINUTES OR LESS
• GLUTEN-FREE OPTION • NUT FREE

I find that when I make one-pot dishes, they are typically in the realm of Italian cuisine. This soup was a nice change from that, plus it shows you just how easy it is to make your own dashi broth. There are a few kinds of dashi, but this is one is based on shiitake mushrooms and kombu! I love that this soup is easy to customize with toppings and seasonings.

FOR THE DASHI BROTH:

8 cups (1.9 L) water
10 dried shiitake mushrooms
1 piece kombu seaweed or
    1 sheet nori

FOR THE ASSEMBLY:

8 ounces (225 g) soba
    noodles, gluten-free if
    desired
2 heads baby bok choy, cut
    into quarters lengthwise
3 ounces (85 g) shiitake
    mushrooms, sliced
¼ cup (60 ml) mirin
¼ cup (60 ml) tamari
1 tablespoon (15 ml) toasted
    sesame oil
1 cup (225 g) diced firm
    silken tofu
¼ cup (25 g) diced green
    onion
2 teaspoons (5 g) toasted
    sesame seeds

To make the broth: Bring the water to a boil in a large pot, then add dried shiitake mushrooms and kombu, adjust heat to medium, cover, and boil for 15 minutes. Remove and discard mushrooms and kombu.

To assemble: Add the soba noodles to the broth and cook for 3 minutes, then add bok choy, and shiitake mushrooms and continue to cook until the noodles are done, 3 to 4 minutes longer. Stir in mirin, tamari, and toasted sesame oil, then divide between four bowls or storage containers. Top each one with tofu, green onion, and sesame seeds and serve warm or store in the refrigerator for up to 7 days.

YIELD: 4 SERVINGS

NUTRITIONAL ANALYSIS
Per serving: 357 calories; 7 g fat; 61 g carbohydrates; 2 g fiber;
8 g sugar; 18 g protein

Tip!
If you like spicy food, use hot chile sesame oil instead of toasted sesame oil.

SESAME MISO STIR-FRY

• *NEEDS SOME HEAT* • *FREEZER FRIENDLY* • *30 MINUTES OR LESS*
• *GLUTEN FREE* • *NUT FREE*

If ever there is a day where you think to yourself, "You know, I haven't really had many vegetables," this dish will totally solve your problem! This beautifully green stir-fry has a variety of veggies and is lightly coated with a simple sesame miso sauce.

2⅔ cups (630 ml) water

1⅓ cups (259 g) short grain white rice

1 tablespoon (15 ml) toasted sesame oil, divided

2 cups (230 g) halved and sliced yellow onion

8 ounces (225 g) baby broccoli or broccolini, cut in half widthwise

2 cups (180 g) chopped green cabbage

2 heads baby bok choy, each sliced into 6 pieces lengthwise

1 tablespoon (15 ml) tamari

1 tablespoon (15 ml) unseasoned rice vinegar

1 tablespoon (16 g) white miso paste

3 cloves garlic, minced

1 teaspoon agave nectar

1 cup (140 g) edamame

Note: The sauce may seem nearly nonexistent at first, but once the sodium from the tamari hits the veggies, they will start to release water, increasing the volume of sauce. If you'd like more of it, just add 2 to 4 tablespoons (30 to 60 ml) water to the sauce before adding it to the skillet.

To make the rice in a multicooker: Place 1⅔ cups (395 ml) water, the rice, and the rice vinegar into the multicooker pot. Bring to high pressure, cooking for 19 minutes, and let sit for 5 minutes, then quick-release the rest of the pressure.

To make the rice on the stovetop: In a pot, bring the water and rice to a boil over medium heat. Cover the pot and adjust the heat to medium-low. Simmer until rice is tender and liquid is absorbed, about 20 minutes. Fluff with a fork and set aside.

To make the stir-fry: In a large skillet or wok, heat 2 teaspoons of the toasted sesame oil over high heat. Add the onions and cook for 2 minutes, stirring occasionally. Add the broccoli, cabbage, and bok choy, to the skillet and cook until there is some browning and the veggies have softened a little, 3 to 5 minutes. Meanwhile, in a small bowl, whisk together the remaining sesame oil and the tamari, rice vinegar, miso paste, garlic, and agave nectar.

Adjust the heat to medium-low and add the sauce and the edamame to the skillet, stirring to coat; cook for 2 more minutes. Divide the rice between 4 bowls or storage containers. Top with the stir-fry and serve immediately, or store in the refrigerator for up to 7 days or in the freezer for up to 3 months.

YIELD: 4 SERVINGS

NUTRITIONAL ANALYSIS
Per serving: 416 calories; 6 g fat; 71 g carbohydrates; 7 g fiber; 8 g sugar; 13 g protein

Chapter 5

HIGHER-PROTEIN MEALS

SATIATING MEALS PACKED WITH DELICIOUS PLANT-SOURCED PROTEINS

Even though it is pretty easy to get the daily recommended amount of protein on a vegan diet, there are some people who want to go above and beyond. These high-protein meals can keep you satiated for longer, offer better recovery from workouts, and help build muscle.

PIÑA COLADA CHIA PUDDING

• FRESH OUTTA THE FRIDGE • UNDER 10 INGREDIENTS
• GLUTEN FREE • NUT FREE • OIL FREE

I've made all kinds of chia puddings over the years, but this was the first time I had added some extra protein via an unexpected ingredient: silken tofu! Honestly, you would never know it's in there; you'll just taste the delicious flavors of coconut and pineapple.

1 (13.5-ounce [400 ml]) can light coconut milk

2½ cups (328 g) chopped pineapple, divided

8 ounces (225 g) silken tofu

½ cup (43 g) unsweetened coconut flakes, divided

3 to 4 tablespoons (45 to 60 ml) agave nectar

½ teaspoon vanilla extract

Pinch salt

¾ cup (132 g) chia seeds

In a blender or a food processor equipped with an S-blade, puree the coconut milk, ½ cup (66 g) of the pineapple, the tofu, ¼ cup (21 g) of the coconut flakes, the agave nectar, the vanilla, and the salt until completely smooth. Add the chia seeds to the mixture and pulse until incorporated but not pureed. Divide the mixture between four bowls or storage containers (I like to use jars here). Top each serving with the remaining pineapple and coconut. Refrigerate for at least 30 minutes or up to 7 days.

YIELD: 4 SERVINGS

NUTRITIONAL ANALYSIS
Per serving: 424 calories; 19 g fat; 49 g carbohydrates; 17 g fiber; 27 g sugar; 17 g protein

Tip!
If you find yourself with a little extra time, toast the coconut flakes for another layer of flavor.

PROTEIN SMOOTHIE BOWLS

- *FREEZER FRIENDLY* • *30 MINUTES OR LESS*
- *GLUTEN FREE* • *NUT FREE* • *OIL FREE*

While ordering smoothie bowls at cafés may be pretty convenient, believe me when I tell you that after you make these, you're going to wish you'd made them at home much sooner—they're so easy and so much less expensive! This recipe is a great base to start with and can easily be modified to suit the season or your taste buds.

FOR THE STOVETOP CRUMBLE:

½ cup (65 g) rolled oats
⅓ cup (40 g) hemp hearts
1½ tablespoons (25 ml) agave nectar
Pinch salt

FOR THE SMOOTHIE BASE:

3 cups (360 g) frozen strawberries
2 bananas, chopped
10 ounces (280 g) frozen dark sweet cherries
1 cup (108 g) vegan vanilla pea protein powder or 4 servings of your favorite protein powder
1 cup (40 g) firmly packed chopped kale
½ cup (120 ml) water
1 lemon, peeled, seeds removed

FOR THE ASSEMBLY:

2 bananas, sliced
1 cup (140 g) sliced fresh strawberries

To make the stovetop crumble: Toast the oats in a dry skillet over medium-low heat for 3 minutes (they will still be light in color). Stir in the hemp hearts, agave nectar, and salt and cook until the mixture starts clumping, 1 to 2 minutes longer. Remove from heat and set aside.

To make the smoothie base: Puree the strawberries, bananas, cherries, protein powder, kale, water, and lemon in a food processor equipped with an S-blade until completely, scraping down the sides as needed (you may need to do this in two batches depending on the size of your processor).

To assemble: Divide the smoothie base between 4 bowls or storage containers, then top with sliced bananas, strawberries, and stovetop crumble. Serve immediately, or store in the freezer for up to 3 months. Let the frozen smoothie bowl defrost in the fridge overnight, then stir well before serving.

YIELD: 4 SERVINGS

NUTRITIONAL ANALYSIS
Per serving: 328 calories; 4 g fat; 56 g carbohydrates; 8 g fiber; 31 g sugar; 24 g protein

BRUSSELS CARROT QUICHE

• *NEEDS SOME HEAT* • *FREEZER FRIENDLY* • *GLUTEN-FREE OPTION*
• *NUT FREE* • *NO SUGAR ADDED*

I may be the author of a few cookbooks, but I am not above making my, or your, life easier with this store-bought pie crust. Homemade crust is great, but the premade version can be a lifesaver on busy days! This delicious quiche is the perfect week-night dinner.

1 (14-ounce [397 g]) package firm tofu, drained and gently pressed

3 tablespoons (25 g) Vegan Eggy Seasoning (page 169)

2 tablespoons (30 ml) plain unsweetened nondairy milk

1 tablespoon (15 ml) olive oil

1 teaspoon onion powder

1 cup (88 g) shaved Brussels sprouts

1 cup (60 g) grated carrots

Salt

Black pepper

1 (9-inch [23 cm]) pie crust, gluten-free if desired

Preheat the oven to 350°F (180°C, or gas mark 4). In a large bowl, combine the tofu, Vegan Eggy Seasoning, nondairy milk, oil, and onion powder. Mash the mixture with a fork or pastry cutter until the chunks are small, but not a paste. Fold in the Brussels sprouts and carrots, season with salt and pepper to taste, then set aside.

Bake the pie crust for 10 minutes. Remove from oven and transfer the filling mixture to the pie crust. Spread the filling into an even layer and press it down flat. Bake for 45 minutes, until the top is matte and golden in color and the crust has some browning. Let cool on a rack for 15 minutes before cutting and serving. Serve immediately or divide between 4 airtight containers and store in the refrigerator for up to 7 days or in the freezer for up to 3 months.

YIELD: 4 SERVINGS

NUTRITIONAL ANALYSIS
Per serving: 402 calories; 28 g fat; 28 g carbohydrates; 7 g fiber; 3 g sugar; 18 g protein

Note: I don't usually have a hard time finding vegan pie crusts in the freezer section of the grocery store because many are made with just shortening and flour, but always double-check the ingredients for dairy products!

CHIPOTLE TEMPEH KALE BOWLS

- **NEEDS SOME HEAT** • **FREEZER FRIENDLY**
- **GLUTEN FREE** • **NUT FREE** • **NO SUGAR ADDED**

Tempeh is one of my favorite vegan proteins. With its nutty taste, basic ingredients, and versatility, how could it not be? Covering it in delicious spices and pairing it with quinoa and my creamy White Bean Garlic Spread (page 162) makes for a tasty, protein-packed dish.

FOR THE QUINOA:

2 cups (475 ml) vegetable broth

1 cup (170 g) tricolor quinoa, rinsed

3 cups (120 g) firmly packed kale, stemmed and torn into bite-size pieces

FOR THE TEMPEH:

2 (8-ounce [225 g]) packages tempeh, cut into 1-inch (2.5 cm) cubes

1½ teaspoons (4 g) onion powder

1 teaspoon garlic powder

½ teaspoon chipotle chile powder

½ teaspoon salt

¼ teaspoon black pepper

1 tablespoon (15 ml) sunflower oil

1 tablespoon (15 ml) lemon juice

FOR THE ASSEMBLY:

½ cup (123 g) White Bean Garlic Spread (page 162)

¼ cup (25 g) diced green onion

4 lemon wedges

To make the quinoa: Combine the vegetable broth and quinoa in a large pot and bring it to a simmer over medium-low heat. Cover and cook for 20 minutes. Remove the pot from the heat, add the kale, and cover so the kale can steam in the residual heat. When the leaves are bright green, remove the lid and set aside.

To make the tempeh: While the quinoa is cooking, arrange the tempeh in a large sauté pan. Add water until it is about ¼ inch (6 mm) high. Cover, bring to a gentle simmer, and cook for 7 minutes to mitigate the tempeh's bitterness. Once tender, drain the water and transfer the tempeh to a bowl.

Stir the onion powder, garlic powder, chipotle chile powder, salt, and black pepper into the tempeh until evenly coated. Heat the sunflower oil in the same large sauté pan over medium heat. Add the tempeh back to pan and cook until the edges begin to brown, about 7 minutes. (You may need to do this in two batches depending on the size of the pan.) Remove the pan from the heat, stir in the lemon juice, and season with salt to taste.

To assemble: Divide the quinoa and kale and the tempeh between 4 bowls or storage containers. Top each bowl with 2 tablespoons (30 g) White Bean Garlic Spread, green onions, and one lemon wedge. Serve warm, or store containers in the refrigerator for up to 7 days.

YIELD: 4 SERVINGS

NUTRITIONAL ANALYSIS
Per serving: 540 calories; 21 g fat; 63 g carbohydrates; 10 g fiber; 7 g sugar; 31 g protein

Tip!
If you made a full batch of the White Bean Garlic Spread for this recipe, you can eat the rest as a snack by cutting up fresh veggies for dipping.

ALMOND BUTTER TOFU STEW

- **NEEDS SOME HEAT** • **FREEZER FRIENDLY**
- **GLUTEN FREE** • **NO SUGAR ADDED**

What's this? *Almond Butter Stew?* Why, yes! This recipe was inspired by west African groundnut stews, but I opted for the peanut-free route. And of course I added kale too, because I'm me, and we could all use a little more kale in our lives.

Tip!
If you're allergic to almonds, use sunflower butter.

FOR THE RICE:

2 cups (475 ml) water
1 cup (185 g) long grain white rice, rinsed

FOR THE STEW:

2 teaspoons (10 ml) sunflower oil
2 cups (240 g) chopped yellow onion
1 cup (150 g) chopped red bell pepper, stem and seeds removed
1 (14-ounce [395 g]) package extra-firm tofu, cut into ¾-inch (2 cm) cubes
1 pound (455 g) sweet potatoes, washed well and chopped
1 cup (160 g) chopped tomatoes
1 tablespoon (8 g) grated fresh ginger
3 cloves garlic, minced
½ cup (165 g) smooth almond butter
¼ cup (64 g) tomato paste
½ teaspoon ground coriander
⅛ teaspoon cayenne pepper, optional
3 cups (710 ml) vegetable broth
4 bay leaves
1 cup (40 g) firmly packed chopped kale
Salt
¼ cup (4 g) loosely packed cilantro leaves
4 lime wedges

To make the rice: In a medium pot, bring the water and rice to a boil. Adjust the heat to medium-low and simmer, covered, until all of the liquid is absorbed and the grains are fluffy, 15 to 20 minutes. Remove the pot from the heat, fluff the rice with a fork, and leave the lid vented.

To make the stew: While the rice is cooking, heat the oil in a large pot over medium heat. Add the onion and bell pepper and cook until the onion starts to soften, about 3 minutes. Push the onion mixture to the side of the pot and add the tofu to the empty space. Cook for 3 minutes, stirring occasionally, then stir in the sweet potatoes, tomatoes, ginger, and garlic and cook, covered, for another 5 minutes.

Add the almond butter, tomato paste, coriander, and cayenne, if using, stirring until evenly combined. Stir in the vegetable broth, add the bay leaves, cover the pot, and bring to a boil. Adjust the heat to medium-low and simmer until the sweet potatoes are easily pierced with a fork, about 15 minutes.

Remove the pot from the heat and discard the bay leaves. Stir in the kale and let it wilt for 1 to 2 minutes. Season with salt to taste. Divide the stew into 4 bowls or storage containers and serve with cilantro and lime wedges. The stew and rice can be stored in the refrigerator for up to 5 days or in the freezer for up to 3 months.

YIELD: 4 SERVINGS

NUTRITIONAL ANALYSIS
Per serving: 633 calories; 27 g fat; 73 g carbohydrates; 13 g fiber; 16 g sugar; 28 g protein

PENNE BOLOGNESE

• NEEDS SOME HEAT • FREEZER FRIENDLY
• GLUTEN FREE • SOY-FREE OPTION

If you're looking for a satiating, warm hug on a plate, this Penne Bolognese is where it's at. A sauce so hearty and flavorful that even my nonvegan, very picky boyfriend gave me an enthusiastic, "I really like this." Know that the protein content will change depending on the pasta you use.

10 ounces (280 g) legume- or quinoa-based penne pasta
1 tablespoon (15 ml) olive oil, plus more for tossing with pasta
1 (15-ounce [425 g]) can tomato sauce
1 batch Pizza Sauce (page 157)
½ teaspoon dried basil
½ teaspoon garlic powder
1 batch Lentil Walnut Sausage Crumbles (page 160)
1 tablespoon (3 g) fresh basil, chiffonade cut

Cook the pasta according to the package's instructions, then drain and rinse with cold water. (If you are prepping this for later, toss the pasta in a very small amount of olive oil to keep it from clumping.) While the pasta is cooking, bring the olive oil, tomato sauce, Pizza Sauce, dried basil, and garlic powder to a simmer in a large saucepan over medium heat, stirring occasionally. Cook until the flavors have melded, about 5 minutes. Reduce heat to low.

Gently fold the Lentil Walnut Sausage Crumbles into the sauce and cook until warmed through. Divide the pasta and sauce between 4 bowls or storage containers and top each with fresh basil. Serve warm, or store in the refrigerator for up to 7 days or in the freezer for up to 3 months.

YIELD: 4 SERVINGS

NUTRITIONAL ANALYSIS
Per serving: 689 calories; 27 g fat; 82 g carbohydrates; 16 g fiber; 14 g sugar; 32 g protein

If you are crunched for time, you can use 12 ounces (340 g) store-bought vegan crumbles in place of the homemade Lentil Walnut Sausage Crumbles!

PINTO PECAN LETTUCE BOATS

• FRESH OUTTA THE FRIDGE • 30 MINUTES OR LESS
• GLUTEN FREE • SOY FREE • NO SUGAR ADDED

Mexican flavors are my jam! But sometimes the tortillas seem too heavy. When I'm craving a meal that's a little lighter, but with all the flavors I love, I make lettuce boats! These puppies have the most delicious filling that comes together with just a blitz in a food processor.

1½ cups (180 g) raw pecans

¾ cup (100 g) chopped red onion

1 tablespoon (8 g) chili powder

1½ teaspoons (4 g) ground cumin

½ to ¾ teaspoon salt

½ teaspoon ground coriander

Pinch cayenne pepper

2 (15-ounce [425 g]) cans pinto beans, drained and rinsed

2 teaspoons sunflower oil

8 large or 12 smaller romaine lettuce leaves

1 avocado, diced

½ cup (105 g) salsa

¼ cup (55 g) Sunflower Sour Cream (page 166) or store-bought vegan sour cream, optional

2 tablespoons (3 g) chopped cilantro

In a food processor equipped with an S-blade, pulse the pecans, onion, chili powder, cumin, salt, coriander, and cayenne until the pecans are broken into pea-size pieces. Add the pinto beans and pulse a couple of times until they have broken down to roughly one-quarter of their original size.

Heat the oil in a large sauté pan over medium heat. Add the pecan-pinto mixture and cook, stirring occasionally and breaking up the big chunks, until there is some browning on the crumbles, 3 to 5 minutes.

To serve right away, divide the filling between the romaine lettuce leaves, then top each one with avocado, salsa, Sunflower Sour Cream, if using, and cilantro. If prepping for later, store the lettuce leaves, filling, and toppings separately in the refrigerator for up to 7 days. Reheat the filling before serving if desired.

YIELD: 4 SERVINGS

NUTRITIONAL ANALYSIS
Per serving: 621 calories; 41 g fat; 51 g carbohydrates; 19 g fiber; 7 g sugar; 20 g protein

If you made a whole batch of Sunflower Sour Cream for this recipe, use the rest of it for topping the Nacho Potato Bake (page 97), or the Barley Beet Borscht (page 128).

*Tip!
If the lettuce boats seem a little unruly, just chop up the romaine and serve this as a taco salad!*

SEITAN FUSION TACOS

• NEEDS SOME HEAT • 30 MINUTES OR LESS • NUT FREE • NO SUGAR ADDED

Love taco Tuesday, but running out of ideas to spice things up? Make these Seitan Fusion Tacos! With wonderful Korean-inspired flavors that magically come together in a toasted corn tortilla, you can't go wrong.

1 tablespoon (15 ml) toasted sesame oil

16 ounces (455 g) Seitan Cutlets (page 168) or store-bought seitan, sliced into ½-inch (1 cm) thick strips

2 tablespoons (30 ml) tamari

1½ tablespoons (25 ml) agave nectar

3 garlic cloves, minced

¼ teaspoon black pepper

12 small corn tortillas

1½ cups (225 g) vegan kimchi, drained

1½ cups (65 g) mung bean sprouts

½ cup (110 g) Gochujang Aioli (page 161)

¼ cup (25 g) diced green onions

If you don't eat gluten, try steaming 16 ounces (455 g) of tempeh, cubing it, then following the seitan prep directions here for a gluten-free alternative.

Heat the oil in a large sauté pan over medium heat. Add the seitan to the pan and cook until the edges are browned, about 6 minutes, flipping halfway through. In a small ramekin or bowl, whisk together the tamari, agave nectar, garlic, and black pepper and pour the mixture over the seitan. Cook until the mixture has caramelized, 1 to 2 minutes.

Warm the tortillas in the microwave or one at a time over a gas stove burner until pliable. Divide the seitan between the tortillas, then top each taco with kimchi, bean sprouts, a drizzle of Gochujang Aioli, and green onions. Serve warm or store in 4 airtight containers in the refrigerator for up to 5 days. If reheating throughout the week, consider storing the kimchi and bean sprouts separately until the tacos are reheated.

YIELD: 4 SERVINGS

NUTRITIONAL ANALYSIS

Per serving: 463 calories; 12g fat; 59 g carbohydrates; 6 g fiber; 8 g sugar; 30 g protein

Tip! If you make a whole batch of the Seitan Cutlets, freeze the leftovers for future recipes or make a batch of the Seitan Jerky (page 148)!

TERIYAKI TOFU WITH CAULIFLOWER FRIED RICE

• NEEDS SOME HEAT • 30 MINUTES OR LESS
• GLUTEN FREE • NUT FREE

On days when I just don't feel like cooking, take-out is a handy solution. Two of my go-tos are fried rice and any teriyaki dish—always vegan, of course. So meal-prepping this Teriyaki Tofu with Cauliflower Fried Rice feels like a veggie-filled take-out indulgence—there when you need it without picking up the phone.

FOR THE CAULIFLOWER FRIED RICE:

2 pounds (907 g) cauliflower, chopped

1 tablespoon (15 ml) toasted sesame oil

4 cloves garlic, minced

1½ cups (195 g) frozen peas and carrots mix

2 tablespoons (30 ml) tamari

Salt

FOR THE TERIYAKI TOFU:

1 tablespoon (15 ml) sunflower oil, divided

16 ounces (455 g) high-protein tofu, cubed

1 cup (120 g) slivered red onion

1 green bell pepper, stemmed, seeded, and sliced

1 red bell pepper, stemmed, seeded, and sliced

1 cup (235 ml) Ginger Teriyaki Sauce (page 156)

To make the cauliflower rice: Pulse the cauliflower in a food processor equipped with an S-blade until it is broken down into roughly rice-sized pieces (you may need to do this in two batches depending on the size of your processor). Transfer the cauliflower to a bowl lined with a kitchen towel. Bring up the edges of the towel and squeeze the cauliflower to remove excess moisture.

Heat the sesame oil in a large pan over high heat. Add the cauliflower, garlic, and peas and carrots and cook for 7 to 9 minutes. Don't stir too often or it may get mushy. In the last minute of cooking, stir in the tamari. Season with salt to taste.

To make the teriyaki tofu: While the cauliflower rice is cooking, heat ½ tablespoon of the sunflower oil in a large sauté pan over medium-high heat. Add the tofu and cook, stirring occasionally, until browned on a few sides, about 10 minutes. Transfer the tofu to a plate, and heat the remaining ½ tablespoon sunflower oil over medium-high heat. Add the onion and bell peppers and cook for 5 minutes, stirring halfway through.

Stir the tofu back in, then stir in the Ginger Teriyaki Sauce. Cook until warmed through, about 2 minutes. Divide the cauliflower rice between 4 bowls or storage containers, top with the stir-fry, and serve warm or store in the refrigerator for up to 7 days.

YIELD: 4 SERVINGS

NUTRITIONAL ANALYSIS
Per serving: 385 calories; 14 g fat; 45 g carbohydrates; 10 g fiber; 25 g sugar; 23 g protein

Tip!
If serving right away, coat the tofu in ¼ cup (40 g) brown rice flour before frying for some added crispy texture.

CITRUS LENTIL QUINOA SALAD

• FRESH OUTTA THE FRIDGE • GLUTEN FREE • SOY FREE

While this salad is great for a weekday lunch, it also doubles as something you can bring to a party as a side—which one of my recipe testers did, to great reception! The lentils and quinoa make this salad filling, and it has a great variety of textures from the lettuce, pistachios, creamy avocado, and orange slices.

¾ cup (144 g) green lentils, rinsed

Salt

1 cup (132 g) quinoa, rinsed

1 pound (455 g) butter lettuce (about 2 heads), chopped

1 cup (160 g) peeled and chopped oranges

1 cup (123 g) chopped roasted pistachios

1 cup (145 g) diced avocado

½ cup (60 g) halved and sliced red onion

1 batch Citrus Vinaigrette (page 159)

Black pepper

In a large pot, combine the lentils and ½ teaspoon salt with 2 cups (475 ml) water. Bring to a boil, then adjust the heat to medium-low and simmer, with vented lid, until the lentils are tender, 25 to 30 minutes. Drain and spread the lentils out over half of a large baking sheet to cool.

While the lentils are cooking, combine the quinoa with 2 cups (475 ml) water in a separate large pot. Bring to a boil, then adjust the heat to medium-low and simmer, covered, until the grains have soaked up the liquid and are fluffy, 15 to 20 minutes. Spread the quinoa out over the other half of the baking sheet to cool. You can place the sheet in the refrigerator to expedite the cooling process.

In a large bowl, combine the lettuce, oranges, pistachios, avocado, and red onion. Add the cooled lentils and quinoa and the Citrus Vinaigrette and toss to combine. Season with salt and black pepper to taste. Chill in the refrigerator for at least 20 minutes before serving in 4 bowls. If storing for later, divide mixture between 4 airtight containers and refrigerate for up to 5 days (there may be some browning on the avocado).

YIELD: 4 SERVINGS

NUTRITIONAL ANALYSIS
Per serving: 454 calories; 21 g fat; 60 g carbohydrates; 15 g fiber; 10 g sugar; 17 g protein

Tip!
Instead of peeling the orange with your hands, carefully slice off the skin with a paring knife, then chop up the fruit.

Chapter 6

SHEET PAN, INSTANT POT, AND FREEZER MEALS

CONVENIENT MEALS USING SOME OF MY FAVORTE KITCHEN TOOLS AND TRICKS!

The whole point of prepping and planning is to save time, make recipes more efficiently, and be ready for whatever comes your way. Making meals using sheet pans, Instant Pots, or slow cookers—and making them freezer friendly—is the epitome of that!

BLOOD ORANGE FREEZER WAFFLES WITH BERRY COMPOTE

• NEEDS SOME HEAT • FREEZER FRIENDLY • 30 MINUTES OR LESS
• GLUTEN-FREE OPTION • SOY FREE • NUT FREE

I have some waffle recipes in my first two books, and I couldn't stop the trend now! Waffles are a terrific make-ahead breakfast because they freeze wonderfully and can be quickly warmed to perfection in the toaster. Paired with a berry compote, these citrusy waffles will put a pep in anyone's step.

FOR THE WAFFLES:

¾ cup (175 ml) blood orange juice plus 1 teaspoon zest

¾ cup (175 ml) plain unsweetened nondairy milk

1¼ cups (156 g) unbleached all-purpose flour or gluten-free flour

½ cup (78 g) rolled oats

3 tablespoons (37 g) sugar

2 tablespoons (30 ml) olive oil

2 teaspoons (9 g) baking powder

2 teaspoons (10 ml) vanilla extract

¼ teaspoon salt

⅛ teaspoon ground cinnamon

FOR THE BERRY COMPOTE:

1½ cups (195 g) blueberries

1 cup (125 g) raspberries

1–2 tablespoons (11–24 g) sugar

1 tablespoon (15 ml) lemon juice

To make the waffles: Preheat a standard waffle maker (not a Belgian waffle maker). Pour the orange juice and zest and the nondairy milk into a blender, followed by the flour, oats, sugar, olive oil, baking powder, vanilla, salt, and cinnamon. Puree until smooth, then allow to rest for 5 minutes to thicken. Cook the waffles according to your waffle maker's instructions.

To make the berry compote: Meanwhile, in a small saucepan, combine the blueberries, raspberries, sugar, and lemon juice and cook over medium heat until they are simmering. Adjust the heat to medium-low, cover, and simmer, stirring occasionally, until the fruit has softened, about 5 minutes. Mash gently with a spoon and simmer for another 2 minutes, uncovered, then set aside.

Serve the waffles warm, topped with berry compote, or allow them to cool to room temperature, transfer to a zip-top bag or storage container, and freeze for up to 3 months. Individual servings of berry compote can be frozen separately.

YIELD: 4 SERVINGS

NUTRITIONAL ANALYSIS
Per serving: 388 calories; 9 g fat;
69 g carbohydrates; 6 g fiber;
27 g sugar; 8 g protein

Tip!
Frozen berries work beautifully in this recipe. I recommend buying frozen fruit in bulk and using it year-round, instead of spending extra for out-of-season produce.

If blood oranges are hard to find at your local store, standard oranges will work just fine!

SPRINGTIME SHEET PAN POLENTA PIZZA

• NEEDS SOME HEAT • GLUTEN FREE • SOY-FREE OPTION

I love me some pizza! For Corey and me, pizza has its own food group. While I am enamored with making my own yeasted pizza dough, this polenta crust saves hours of my time and is more allergy friendly. Is it quite as crispy? No, but the flavors are incredible, and the hearty polenta is perfectly satiating.

If you are storing this for later, I recommend placing two slices in each storage container with a piece of parchment paper between them.

FOR THE POLENTA CRUST:

2 cups (475 ml) water
2 cups (475 ml) vegetable broth
1½ cups (230 g) polenta grits
3 tablespoons (15 g) nutritional yeast
Salt
Cooking spray

FOR THE TOPPINGS:

1 batch Pizza Sauce (page 157)
1 cup (105 g) vegan mozzarella shreds
½ batch Lentil Walnut Sausage Crumbles (page 160)
1 cup (100 g) thinly sliced fennel
1 cup (80 g) 2-inch (5 cm) long asparagus spears, woody ends removed
½ cup (30 g) 2-inch (5 cm) long green onion pieces
¼ cup (29 g) thinly sliced radishes
Cooking spray

Preheat the oven to 400°F (200°C, or gas mark 6), and line a large baking sheet with parchment paper (do not use a silicone mat here). In a pot, combine water, vegetable broth, polenta grits, and nutritional yeast and bring mixture to a boil over medium-high heat. Reduce the heat to low, and cook with vented lid, stirring occasionally, until the polenta is creamy and soft, 18 to 20 minutes. Season with salt to taste.

Carefully pour the polenta onto the prepared baking sheet and spread it into an 11 x 15-inch (28 x 38 cm) rectangle that is about ½ inch (1 cm) thick. Spray lightly with cooking spray, then bake for 20 minutes. Carefully flip the crust over by laying a second sheet of parchment paper on top of the crust followed by an upside-down cooling rack; hold the sheet and rack securely together and flip them over. Discard the original parchment (which should now be on top of the polenta) and carefully slide the crust, still on the second sheet of parchment, back onto the baking sheet. Bake for another 10 minutes, then remove from the oven (but don't turn the oven off).

Spread the Pizza Sauce over the crust in an even layer. Top with the vegan mozzarella shreds, then the Lentil Walnut Sausage Crumbles, fennel, asparagus, green onion, and radishes. Spray lightly with cooking spray and bake for another 15 minutes, until the toppings have started to brown. Let cool for 7 to 10 minutes before slicing into 8 pieces and serving. Pizza can be stored for up to 7 days in the refrigerator.

YIELD: 4 SERVINGS

NUTRITIONAL ANALYSIS
Per serving: 515 calories; 17 g fat; 74 g carbohydrates; 13 g fiber; 12 g sugar; 15 g protein

And another thing! If you have an air fryer at home, use it to reheat this pizza at 350°F (180°C) for 7 minutes.

INSTANT POT BARBECUE SOY CURL SANDWICHES

• NEEDS SOME HEAT • 30 MINUTES OR LESS
• GLUTEN-FREE OPTION • NUT FREE

If you've never heard of soy curls, get ready to try one of my favorite vegan proteins! Just as versatile as tofu in that it soaks up whatever flavors you dress it with, but with a texture that makes it a great vegan substitute for chicken.

FOR THE BARBECUE SOY CURLS:

2 teaspoons (10 ml) sunflower oil

1 cup (140 g) diced yellow onion

3 cups (180 g) dry soy curls

1 cup (240 g) Veggie Barbecue Sauce (page 164) or store-bought vegan barbecue sauce

1 cup (235 ml) vegetable broth or vegan chicken broth

1 teaspoon smoked paprika

½ teaspoon black pepper

FOR THE ASSEMBLY:

2 cups (180 g) shredded green cabbage

1 cup (90 g) shredded red cabbage

1 tablespoon (15 ml) apple cider vinegar

2 teaspoons (10 ml) agave nectar

½ teaspoon salt

1/8 teaspoon black pepper

¼ cup (55 g) vegan mayo (optional)

4 burger buns or sandwich rolls, gluten free if desired

To make the barbecue soy curls: Using the sauté function of your Instant Pot or multicooker, heat the oil. Add the onions and cook for 5 minutes, stirring occasionally. Stir in the soy curls, ½ cup (120 g) of the Veggie Barbecue Sauce, vegetable broth, smoked paprika, and black pepper. Close the lid and bring to high pressure. Once the pot reaches high pressure, cook for 7 minutes, then turn off the heat and quick-release the pressure. Stir in the remaining barbecue sauce; keep on the warm setting.

To assemble: While the soy curls are cooking, toss together the green cabbage, red cabbage, apple cider vinegar, agave nectar, salt, and pepper in a large bowl and refrigerate until ready to make the sandwiches. To assemble, spread the vegan mayo, if using, on each bun, then top with barbecue soy curls and slaw. Serve warm or wrap the sandwiches in paper and store in the refrigerator for up to 5 days.

YIELD: 4 SERVINGS

NUTRITIONAL ANALYSIS
Per serving: 356 calories; 22 g fat; 47 g carbohydrates; 7 g fiber; 15 g sugar; 17 g protein

Note: Soy curls are soybeans that have been extruded and dehydrated. Unlike textured vegetable protein (TVP), soy curls still have some of the fiber from the beans. They can be found in some natural food stores or ordered online. If you can't find them, use TVP instead!

HEARTY SPINACH LASAGNA

• NEEDS SOME HEAT • FREEZER FRIENDLY • GLUTEN-FREE OPTION

Every year my dude's grandmother has the whole family over for Christmas and makes lasagna. A year or two after I went vegan, she started making a little batch just for me, which honestly means so much. Of course, because of years of his grandmother's lasagna, my dude has become a connoisseur of sorts, so I knew I had to put some serious effort into a hearty vegan version. Verdict: It's an absolute success!

FOR THE TOFU RICOTTA:

2 (14-ounce [397 g]) pack-ages firm tofu, drained

1 cup (137 g) raw cashews

¼ cup (60 ml) lemon juice

2 tablespoons (14 g) refined coconut oil

2 tablespoons (32 g) white miso paste

3 cloves garlic

1 teaspoon salt, or to taste

FOR THE SAUCE:

2 teaspoons (10 ml) sun-flower oil

1 large yellow onion, diced

4 cloves garlic, minced

3 tablespoons (48 g) tomato paste

1 (28-ounce [794 g]) can tomato sauce

1 (28-ounce [794 g]) can crushed tomatoes

2 to 3 teaspoons (8 to 12 g) sugar

1 teaspoon dried basil

¾ teaspoon dried oregano

½ teaspoon dried parsley

(continued)

To make the tofu ricotta: Press the tofu in a tofu press or by wrapping it in a kitchen towel and setting a flat, heavy object on top of it to press out some of the moisture. Let it sit for 15 minutes, then transfer to a food processor equipped with an S-blade, followed by the cashews, lemon juice, coconut oil, miso paste, garlic, and salt. Process the mixture until completely smooth, then transfer to a container and store in the refrigerator.

To make the sauce: Meanwhile, in a large pot, heat the oil over medium-low heat. Add the onion and cook until it starts to become translucent, about 5 minutes. Add the garlic and tomato paste and cook until fragrant. Stir in the tomato sauce, crushed tomatoes, sugar, basil, oregano, parsley, and black pepper, cover, and simmer for 15 minutes, stirring occasionally. Add the red wine vinegar, season with salt to taste, then remove from the heat and cover to keep warm.

To assemble: Preheat the oven to 350°F (180°C, or gas mark 4). Cook the lasagna noodles according to the package's instructions then lay the cooked noodles out flat on a baking sheet.

Spread 1 cup (245 g) of the tomato sauce in the bottom of a 10 x 15-inch (25 x 38-cm) baking dish. Top the sauce with one layer of lasagna noodles, covering the bottom of the dish as completely as you can. Spread another 2 cups (490 g) of tomato sauce over the noodles, then top with half of the spinach, and one-third of the Lentil Walnut Sausage Crumbles.

(continued)

(continued)

¼ teaspoon black pepper

2 teaspoons (10 ml) red wine vinegar

Salt

FOR THE ASSEMBLY:

16 ounces (455 g) lasagna noodles, gluten free if desired

16 ounces (455 g) frozen chopped spinach, thawed

1 batch Lentil Walnut Sausage Crumbles (page 160)

¼ cup (10 g) chiffonade-cut basil

Note: Don't have a big enough casserole dish on hand? Most grocery stores have large foil pans just for this purpose!

Set aside ½ cup (135 g) of the tofu ricotta. Spoon half of the remaining ricotta over the crumbles, then top with another layer of lasagna noodles, pressing down gently to flatten the ricotta. Spoon another 2 cups (490 g) of tomato sauce over the noodles, followed by the remaining spinach, and half of the remaining Lentil Walnut Sausage Crumbles. Dollop the other half of the ricotta over the layers, and top with a layer of noodles, pressing down gently. Finally, top with remaining tomato sauce and Lentil Walnut Sausage Crumbles, then dollop the reserved ½ cup (135 g) of ricotta over the top. Bake the lasagna for 35 to 40 minutes, until bubbling.

Let cool on a rack for 20 minutes before topping with fresh basil. Serve warm or divide into eight storage containers and store in the refrigerator for up to 7 days or in the freezer for up to 3 months.

YIELD: 8 SERVINGS

NUTRITIONAL ANALYSIS
Per serving: 726 calories; 31 g fat; 81 g carbohydrates; 11 g fiber; 12 g sugar; 31 g protein

*Tip!
To save a little time, you can use 14 ounces (397 g) of store-bought vegan crumbles in place of the Lentil Walnut Sausage Crumbles.*

INSTANT POT BOUILLABAISSE

• NEEDS SOME HEAT • FREEZER FRIENDLY • GLUTEN FREE
• SOY FREE • NUT FREE • NO SUGAR ADDED

Sometimes I need some recipe inspiration to kickstart my brain a little bit, so I sorted through my vintage box of Betty Crocker recipe cards looking for ideas. Aside from some of the monstrosities I found, I looked over a card for bouillabaisse and knew that I could easily veganize this seafood stew using some delicious mushrooms. I didn't really follow that recipe, but developed a dish that's reminiscent of traditional French cuisine, only vegan and made speedier with a multicooker!

> **Tip!**
> Save those odds and ends from the onion, leeks, and mushroom stems to use in the Vegetable Scrap Broth (page 165)!

1 tablespoon (15 ml) sunflower oil

2 cups (178 g) chopped leeks, coarse green parts removed

1 fennel bulb, cored and chopped, fronds reserved

½ cup (70 g) diced yellow onion

¼ cup (35 g) diced shallots

4 cups (945 ml) vegetable broth, divided

2 (14.5-ounce [411 g]) cans whole peeled tomatoes, halved, seeded, and drained

3 bay leaves

12 ounces (340 g) king oyster mushrooms, sliced into 1-inch (2.5 cm) round slices

7 ounces (200 g) maitake or oyster mushrooms, roughly chopped

1 (15-ounce [425 g]) can white beans, drained and rinsed

1 sheet nori, diced

½ teaspoon dried thyme

½ teaspoon dried marjoram

½ teaspoon fennel seeds

2 tablespoons (30 ml) lemon juice or white wine

Salt

Toasted, sliced baguette for serving (optional)

Using the sauté function of your Instant Pot or multicooker, heat the oil for 1 minute. Add the leeks, fennel, yellow onion, and shallots and cook for 4 minutes, until softened but not browned. Add 3 cups (710 ml) of the vegetable broth, the tomatoes, and the bay leaves. Close the lid and bring to high pressure. Once the pot reaches high pressure, cook for 4 minutes, then turn off the heat and quick-release the pressure. Remove and discard the bay leaves, then, using an immersion blender, partially puree the vegetables until they are in small pieces, but not smooth.

Using a fine sieve or nut milk bag, strain the veggie mixture into a large bowl, pressing or squeezing to get as much liquid out as you can (be careful, as the mixture will be hot). Discard the pulp and set the liquid aside. Add the mushrooms, white beans, nori, thyme, marjoram, fennel seeds, tomato broth, and the remaining vegetable broth to the now-empty multicooker, then close the lid and bring the pot to high pressure. Once the pot reaches high pressure, cook for 4 minutes. Turn off the heat, quick-release the pressure, and stir in the lemon juice. Season with salt to taste. Serve warm with toasted baguette slices, if using, let to cool for 10 minutes and store in the refrigerator for up to 7 days, or store in the freezer for up to 6 months.

YIELD: 4 SERVINGS

NUTRITIONAL ANALYSIS
Per serving (without baguette): 245 calories; 5 g fat; 41 g carbohydrates; 14 g fiber; 12 g sugar; 11 g protein

INSTANT POT CREAMY BROCCOLI SOUP

• NEEDS SOME HEAT • FREEZER FRIENDLY • 30 MINUTES OR LESS
• GLUTEN-FREE OPTION • SOY FREE • NO SUGAR ADDED

Creamy soups are oh-so-comforting, and though this Creamy Broccoli Soup
is on the lighter side, it's still quite a hug in a bowl. Serve this veggie-filled soup
with a crusty sliced of toasted sourdough for the ultimate cold-weather dinner.

1 tablespoon (15 ml) sun-
flower oil

1 cup (140 g) diced yellow
onion

1 cup (130 g) diced carrots

3 cloves garlic, minced

3 cups (285 g) broccoli
florets

1 (15-ounce [425 g]) can
white beans

2 cups (475 ml) vegetable
broth

1 cup (235 ml) plain unsweetened nondairy milk

¼ cup (20 g) nutritional
yeast

¼ cup (31 g) all-purpose
flour or gluten-free flour

2 tablespoons (30 ml) lemon
juice

Salt

Black pepper

4 slices of toasted bread,
gluten-free if desired
(optional)

Using the sauté function of your Instant Pot or multicooker, heat the oil.
Add the onion and cook for 3 minutes, then add the carrots and garlic and
cook for an additional 2 minutes. Stir in the broccoli, white beans with their
liquid, and vegetable broth, close the lid, and bring to high pressure. Once
the pot reaches high pressure, cook for 3 minutes, then turn off the heat and
quick-release the pressure.

Whisk together the nondairy milk, nutritional yeast, and flour, then add the
mixture to the soup base. Using an immersion blender, or working in batches
in a blender, puree half of the soup. Stir in the lemon juice and season with
salt and pepper to taste. Serve with toasted bread, or divide between four
storage containers and store in the refrigerator for up to 7 days or in the
freezer for up to 6 months.

YIELD: 4 SERVINGS

NUTRITIONAL ANALYSIS
Per serving (not including bread): 241 calories;
5 g fat; 37 g carbohydrates; 10 g fiber;
6 g sugar; 13 g protein

Tip!
Save those odds
and ends from the onion
and carrots to use in
the Vegetable
Scrap Broth
(page 165)!

Pictured front to back:
Instant Pot Bouillabaise,
Barley Beet Borscht, and
Creamy Broccoli Soup

INSTANT POT BARLEY BEET BORSCHT

• NEEDS SOME HEAT • FREEZER FRIENDLY • GLUTEN-FREE OPTION
• SOY FREE • NUT FREE • OIL FREE • NO SUGAR ADDED

If you've read either of my previous books, you might remember that half of my family is from Eastern Europe. There's bound to be a few recipes here and there influenced by my heritage, and this is one of them. Though this borscht isn't pureed, it has all the essential flavors plus the satiating addition of barley!

6 cups (1.4 L) vegetable broth, divided

1 cup (200 g) pearled barley or short grain brown rice

2 cups (475 ml) water

2 cups (300 g) peeled and diced red beets

2 cups (280 g) diced red onion

2 cups (180 g) chopped red cabbage

1 cup (100 g) chopped celery

1 cup (130 g) sliced carrots

3 bay leaves

Salt

Black pepper

½ cup (110 g) Sunflower Sour Cream (page 166) or plain vegan yogurt

1 tablespoon (4 g) chopped fresh dill

Combine 1½ cups (355 ml) of the vegetable broth and the barley in an Instant Pot or pressure cooker, then close the lid and bring to high pressure. Once the pot reaches high pressure, cook for 15 minutes, then turn off the heat and quick-release the pressure. Stir in the remaining vegetable broth and the water, beets, onion, cabbage, celery, carrots, and bay leaves. Again, close the lid, bring back up to high pressure, and cook for 3 minutes. Turn off the heat, let the soup sit for 5 minutes, then quick-release the pressure and carefully remove the lid.

Season the soup with salt and black pepper to taste, then divide between four bowls or storage containers. Top each one with the Sunflower Sour Cream and fresh dill just before serving. Soup can be stored in the refrigerator for up to 7 days or in the freezer for up to 3 months.

YIELD: 4 SERVINGS

NUTRITIONAL ANALYSIS
Per serving (including Sunflower Sour Cream):
313 calories; 7 g fat; 59 g carbohydrates;
15 g fiber; 12 g sugar; 10 g protein

Tip!
Save those odds and ends from the onion and carrots to use in the Vegetable Scrap Broth (page 165)!

DILL-ROASTED CHICKPEAS WITH POTATO WEDGES

• NEEDS SOME HEAT • GLUTEN FREE
• SOY FREE • NUT FREE • NO SUGAR ADDED

Sometimes when everything in a meal is roasted, it can become beige and boring in both looks and flavor. Not this sheet-pan dish! Timed just right, you get golden, lemony potatoes, al dente Brussels, and savory chickpeas, all dressed with a perky sour cream sauce.

FOR THE CHICKPEAS:

2 (15-ounce [425 g]) cans chickpeas, drained and rinsed
1/3 cup (45 g) diced yellow onion
2 teaspoons (10 ml) sunflower oil
1 teaspoon dried dill
1/2 teaspoon salt
1/2 teaspoon garlic powder
1/4 teaspoon black pepper

FOR THE POTATOES:

1 pound (455 g) Yukon Gold potatoes, cut into wedges
2 teaspoons (10 ml) sunflower oil
2 teaspoons (4 g) lemon pepper
1/2 teaspoon paprika
Pinch salt
12 ounces (340 g) Brussels sprouts, shaved

FOR THE ASSEMBLY:

1/2 cup (110 g) Sunflower Sour Cream (page 166)
2 tablespoons (30 ml) water
1 tablespoon (3 g) minced chives
2 teaspoons (10 ml) lemon juice
1/4 teaspoon dried dill
Pinch salt
4 lemon wedges

To make the chickpeas: Preheat the oven to 400°F (200°C, or gas mark 6) and line two baking sheets with parchment paper. In a bowl, combine the chickpeas, onion, oil, dill, salt, garlic powder, and pepper, tossing until evenly coated. Spread the mixture out on one of the baking sheets.

To make the potatoes: In a bowl, combine the potatoes, oil, lemon pepper, paprika, and salt, tossing until evenly coated. Spread the wedges out on the other baking sheet in a single layer. Place the baking sheets in the oven and roast for 20 minutes. Flip the potatoes and move the chickpeas to one side of the baking sheet. Spread the Brussels sprouts next to the chickpeas. Put the sheets back in the oven on opposite racks and roast for another 20 minutes.

To assemble: Meanwhile, whisk together Sunflower Sour Cream, water, chives, lemon juice, dried dill, and salt. Refrigerate the sauce until ready to serve. To serve, divide the chickpeas, potatoes, Brussels sprouts, and lemon wedges between 4 bowls or storage containers. Drizzle with sour cream sauce just before serving. The sauce and the dishes can be stored separately in the refrigerator for up to 7 days.

YIELD: 4 SERVINGS

NUTRITIONAL ANALYSIS
Per serving: 442 calories; 11 g fat; 67 g carbohydrates; 13 g fiber; 5 g sugar; 21 g protein

SMOKY TOFU SQUASH SALAD

• FRESH OUTTA THE FRIDGE • GLUTEN FREE • NO SUGAR ADDED

The fall flavors of the roasted squash and onion and the peppery arugula in this salad are so, so good, and it's done with so little active cooking time! I guess that's the great part of sheet pan meals, right? If you don't care for tofu, tempeh or chickpeas would also be great using this method.

FOR THE TOFU AND SQUASH:

1 (14-ounce [397 g]) package extra-firm tofu, drained

1 tablespoon (15 ml) sunflower oil, divided

1 teaspoon smoked paprika

1 teaspoon onion powder

¾ teaspoon salt

½ teaspoon dried oregano

½ teaspoon dry mustard powder

2 pounds (905 g) acorn squash, seeded and chopped

1 cup (120 g) chopped red onion

FOR THE SALAD:

5 ounces (140 g) baby arugula

½ cup (120 ml) Cashew Ranch (page 167)

To make the tofu: Preheat the oven to 400°F (200°C, or gas mark 6) and line a baking sheet with parchment paper. Wrap the tofu in a kitchen towel and gently squeeze to remove excess moisture, then cut it into cubes and transfer to a bowl. Gently stir in ½ tablespoon of the oil, the smoked paprika, onion powder, salt, dried oregano, and mustard powder. Spread over one third of the prepared baking sheet.

In the now-empty bowl, toss the squash, red onion, and remaining ½ tablespoon oil. Spread the mixture over the remainder of the baking sheet. Roast for 1 hour, flipping halfway through roasting. Let cool on a rack for 10 minutes.

To make the salad: Divide the arugula between 4 bowls or storage containers and top with the roasted veggies and tofu. Drizzle with Cashew Ranch just before serving. Store salads and dressing separately in the refrigerator for up to 7 days.

YIELD: 4 SERVINGS

NUTRITIONAL ANALYSIS
Per serving: 262 calories; 10 g fat; 33 g carbohydrates; 6 g fiber; 2 g sugar; 14 g protein

INSTANT POT SPAGHETTI SQUASH WITH PISTACHIO SAGE SAUCE

- **NEEDS SOME HEAT • FREEZER FRIENDLY • 30 MINUTES OR LESS**
- **UNDER 10 INGREDIENTS • GLUTEN FREE • SOY FREE**
- **OIL FREE • NO SUGAR ADDED**

Even though I love spaghetti squash, it usually takes some time to get the dang thing roasted or steamed. Not with this multicooker method! Even with the time it takes to get to pressure, the process is only a fraction of what it would take in the oven—and with a large squash, too!

1 (4-pound [1815 g])
spaghetti squash
1 cup (123 g) shelled raw
pistachios plus ¼ cup
(35 g) chopped roasted
pistachios
2 cups (475 ml) vegetable
broth
1 cup (89 g) chopped leeks
1½ teaspoons (1 g) ground
sage
1 teaspoon dried thyme
½ teaspoon salt
¼ teaspoon black pepper
1 teaspoon red wine vinegar

Cut the spaghetti squash into four round slices, scoop out the seeds, and arrange on a rack in your Instant Pot or multicooker. Add 1 cup (235 ml) water, then close the lid and bring to high pressure. Once the pot reaches high pressure, cook for 7 minutes, then turn off the heat and let sit for 3 minutes before quick-releasing the pressure. Remove the lid and allow the squash to cool for 10 minutes before handling.

While the squash is cooking, put the raw pistachios in a small pot and cover them with water. Bring to a boil, then adjust the heat to medium-low and simmer, covered, for 5 minutes. Drain and rinse the pistachios and transfer them to a blender, adding the vegetable broth, leeks, sage, thyme, salt, and black pepper. Puree until smooth, then let sit for 5 minutes before pureeing again.

Transfer the sauce to a skillet, add the vinegar, and simmer over medium-low heat, stirring occasionally, for 5 minutes. Pull the squash from the skin with a fork and divide it between four bowls or storage containers, then top with the sauce and the roasted pistachios. Serve warm or store in the refrigerator for up to 7 days or in the freezer for up to 3 months.

YIELD: 4 SERVINGS

NUTRITIONAL ANALYSIS
Per serving: 354 calories; 18 g fat; 45 g carbohydrates;
11 g fiber; 17 g sugar; 10 g protein

Chapter 7

KID-FRIENDLY FOODS

MINI FOODS, HIDDEN VEGGIES, FUN SHAPES, AND MORE!

I may not have kids of my own, but I am an official aunt to one nephew and an unofficial aunt to many more children. I think it's safe to say that kids can be pretty finicky, so I've put together some recipes that are easy for you to prep and are a great foundation to build upon, depending on your young child's preferences.

VEGGIE BENTO BOXES

• FRESH OUTTA THE FRIDGE • 30 MINUTES OR LESS
• UNDER 10 INGREDIENTS • GLUTEN FREE • NUT FREE
• OIL FREE • NO SUGAR ADDED

Bento boxes are common in Japanese cuisine and are essentially single-serving meals in compartmentalized containers. These bentos are really simple, with basic cooked rice and sliced veggies. To make these cuter and more eye-catching, use a cherry blossom-shaped cutter to slice the vegetables! You can find them at some Asian markets or outlets.

FOR THE RICE:

1¼ cups (285 ml) water, or
    2 cups (475 ml) if cooking
    rice on stove
1 cup (190 g) short grain
    brown rice
1 tablespoon (15 ml) unsea-
    soned rice vinegar

FOR THE BENTO BOXES:

1 cup (130 g) sliced
    cucumber
1 cup (116 g) peeled and
    sliced daikon radish
1 red bell pepper, stemmed,
    seeded, and diced
1 cup (95 g) shelled and
    cooked edamame
3 sheets nori, each cut into
    4 squares
2 teaspoons (5 g) toasted
    sesame seeds
2 tablespoons (30 ml) tamari

To make the rice in a multicooker: Combine 1¼ cups (285 ml) water, rice, and rice vinegar in a multicooker and bring to high pressure, cook for 19 minutes, let sit for 5 minutes, then quick-release the rest of the pressure. Transfer the rice to a bowl and chill in the refrigerator.

To make the rice on the stovetop: Combine 2 cups (475 ml) water, rice, rice vinegar, and salt in a pot, bring to a boil, then adjust heat to medium-low and simmer, with vented lid, until rice is tender and liquid is absorbed, 30 to 35 minutes. Transfer the rice to a bowl and chill in the refrigerator.

To make the bento boxes: Divide the rice between 4 storage containers with dividers, then top with cucumber, daikon, and red bell pepper. Divide the edamame and nori between additional compartments. Sprinkle sesame seeds over each box and serve with tamari on the side. Store in the refrigerator for up to 5 days.

YIELD: 4 SERVINGS

NUTRITIONAL ANALYSIS
Per serving: 239 calories; 4 g fat;
44 g carbohydrates; 5 g fiber;
4 g sugar; 10 g protein

Tip!
If you want to bulk up this meal a bit, I recommend getting frozen, vegan-friendly spring rolls and adding one to each bento box.

Note: This recipe shares a lot of ingredients with the Mushroom Hand Rolls (page 90), so if you want to make lunch for both you and the kids, you can bulk cook and prepare the ingredients.

BANANA-CHIP MINI MUFFINS

• FRESH OUTTA THE FRIDGE • FREEZER FRIENDLY
• UNDER 10 INGREDIENTS • SOY FREE • NUT FREE

I can't remember how old I was, but when I was a kid, a bakery company came out with snack packages of mini muffins, and I was in love! Blueberry-dotted mini muffins that were the perfect size to pop into your mouth. Here, I have a much less processed version—basically banana bread sans nuts, and super-tasty!

3 tablespoons (45 ml) hot water

1 tablespoon (10 g) chia seeds

¾ cup (94 g) whole wheat flour

1 teaspoon ground cinnamon

1 teaspoon baking soda

¼ teaspoon salt

1 cup (225 g) mashed very ripe banana

½ cup (65 g) loosely packed brown sugar

2 tablespoons (30 ml) olive oil

1 teaspoon vanilla extract

¼ cup (44 g) dairy-free chocolate chips

Preheat oven to 350°F (180°C, or gas mark 4) and line the outer cups of a 24-count mini-muffin pan with 16 liners. In a medium bowl, stir together the hot water and chia seeds and set them aside to gel. In a large bowl, sift together the flour, cinnamon, baking soda, and salt.

Add the banana, sugar, olive oil, and vanilla into the chia seed mixture and whisk until mostly smooth. Add the banana mixture to the flour mixture and fold together until there are no dry pockets. Spoon about 2 tablespoons (30 g) of batter into each of the 16 liners, then top each muffin with a few chocolate chips. Bake for 25 minutes, or until a toothpick inserted in the center of the muffins comes out clean.

Let cool for 10 minutes before removing from the pan. Store in the refrigerator for up to 7 days.

YIELD: ABOUT 16 MINI MUFFINS

NUTRITIONAL ANALYSIS
Per serving (1 muffin): 98 calories; 3 g fat; 17 g carbohydrates; 1 g fiber; 10 g sugar; 1 g protein

VEGGIE QUESADILLAS

• FRESH OUTTA THE FRIDGE • 30 MINUTES OR LESS
• UNDER 10 INGREDIENTS • GLUTEN FREE • SOY FREE
• NUT FREE • NO SUGAR ADDED

Quesadillas were my jam as a kid! Cheesy goodness packed with whatever my sister Katie and I wanted— which wasn't much. I still make quesadillas, but these ones are simple and kid friendly. They take under 20 minutes to make, even with the vegetable grating.

1 cup (120 g) grated zucchini
1 cup (110 g) grated carrot
½ teaspoon salt
8 corn tortillas
1 cup (115 g) vegan cheese shreds
Oil for greasing the pan
1 (15-ounce [425 g]) can vegan refried beans
½ cup (105 g) salsa

Toss the zucchini, carrots, and salt in a strainer set over a bowl; this will draw out some of the vegetables' moisture and avoid soggy quesadillas. Let sit for 5 minutes, then take a kitchen towel or paper towel and press firmly on the vegetables to remove as much liquid as possible. Lay out four of the tortillas, divide the vegan cheese shreds among them, then top with the drained vegetables. Top with the remaining tortillas.

Brush a small skillet with a thin layer of oil, then heat over medium heat. Working with one quesadilla at a time, gently lay the quesadilla in the pan and cook until the cheese shreds are melted, 4 to 6 minutes, flipping halfway through cooking. Repeat with the remaining quesadillas. Let the cooked quesadillas rest for 2 minutes before cutting them into quarters. Divide the quesadillas, refried beans, and salsa between 4 plates or storage containers and serve warm or store in the refrigerator for up to 5 days.

YIELD: 4 SERVINGS

NUTRITIONAL ANALYSIS
Per serving: 329 calories; 10 g fat; 51 g carbohydrates; 11 g fiber; 6 g sugar; 10 g protein

KIDNEY BEAN SLIDERS WITH SWEET POTATO FRIES

• *NEEDS SOME HEAT* • *FREEZER FRIENDLY* • *GLUTEN-FREE OPTION*
• *SOY-FREE OPTION* • *NO SUGAR ADDED*

Everything is cuter when it's miniature, right? Isn't that why so many adults love sliders? They're also the perfect size for a child's lunch box. This patty recipe is a half batch of the Mushroom Onion Burgers (page 103), so you can easily make dinner for yourself and your kid(s) in one fell swoop.

FOR THE BURGERS:
¼ cup (25 g) raw walnuts
¼ cup (25 g) quick-cooking oats
½ teaspoon smoked paprika
½ teaspoon onion powder
½ teaspoon dried parsley
Black pepper
½ can (7.5 ounces [210 g])
    kidney beans, drained and rinsed
¼ cup (35 g) diced yellow onion
¼ cup (18 g) sliced mushrooms
1½ teaspoons (8 ml) olive oil
1½ teaspoons (8 ml) tamari or
    coconut aminos
Salt

FOR THE FRIES:
1 (12-ounce [340 g]) sweet potato, cut into
    3-inch (7.5 cm) long matchsticks
1 tablespoon (15 ml) sunflower oil
Salt

FOR THE ASSEMBLY:
4 teaspoons (21 g) mustard, ketchup,
    or mayonnaise
4 slider-size buns, gluten-free if desired
1 leaf green lettuce, cut into 8 pieces

To make the burgers: Preheat the oven to 375°F (190°C, or gas mark 5) and line a baking sheet with parchment paper. Pulse the walnuts, oats, smoked paprika, onion powder, dried parsley, and ⅛ teaspoon black pepper in a food processor equipped with an S-blade until the walnuts are fine crumbles. Add the beans, onion, mushrooms, olive oil, tamari, and a pinch of salt to the processor and pulse until it forms a dough, being careful not to overprocess into a paste. Form the mixture into four patties and spread them out on one-third of the prepared baking sheet.

To make the fries: Toss the sweet potato with the oil and ½ teaspoon salt and spread out on the other two-thirds of the baking sheet. Bake for 15 minutes, then flip the patties and fries and bake for another 15 minutes. Remove the patties from the baking sheet and return it to the oven to bake for 15 minutes longer, until the fries start to brown on the edges. Sprinkle the fries with salt to taste.

To assemble: Spread the mustard on the insides of the buns. Top with a patty and two lettuce pieces. Serve with fries immediately, or let everything cool to room temperature before storing in the refrigerator for up to 5 days.

YIELD: 4 SERVINGS

NUTRITIONAL ANALYSIS
Per serving: 328 calories; 11 g fat; 49 g carbohydrates; 8 g fiber; 7 g sugar; 11 g protein

DIY MINI PIZZAS

- *FRESH OUTTA THE FRIDGE • 30 MINUTES OR LESS*
- *GLUTEN-FREE OPTION • SOY FREE • NUT FREE*
- *OIL FREE • NO SUGAR ADDED*

When I was in elementary school, I was always envious of the kids who were eating Lunchables, especially the pizza ones. Now, it's time to cater to my inner child with this easy-to-assemble DIY pizza kit. I've listed the basics here, but feel free to customize the toppings according to what your child enjoys.

Tip!
Cut up the extra pita and toast the pieces in the oven, in an air fryer, or on the stove to use as chips.

3 pitas or 6 gluten-free tortillas

½ batch Pizza Sauce (page 157)

1 cup (115 g) vegan mozzarella shreds or 1 cup (246 g) White Bean Garlic Spread (page 162)

1 cup (70 g) thinly sliced mushrooms

1 cup (30 g) chopped spinach

¼ cup (25 g) sliced black olives

Using a 3-inch (7.5 cm) circular cutter, cut 4 circles out of each pita and split layers to make 24 crusts. Divide the crusts between four storage containers with dividers. Divide the Pizza Sauce, vegan mozzarella shreds, mushrooms, spinach, and black olives between the containers. Store in the refrigerator for up to 5 days.

YIELD: 4 SERVINGS

NUTRITIONAL ANALYSIS
Per serving: 262 calories; 9 g fat; 45 g carbohydrates; 6 g fiber; 5 g sugar; 8 g protein

Part 4

BASICS AND BONUSES

Chapter 8

SNACK ATTACK!

THIS MAY BE A MEAL PREP BOOK, BUT SNACKS ARE A MUST-HAVE FOR HOLDING YOU OVER IN BETWEEN.

Though my blog's name, *Vegan Yack Attack*, stemmed from my name, Jackie, it may as well have been Vegan *Snack* Attack, because I absolutely adore snacks. In this chapter there is a wide variety of sweet, savory, healthy, and indulgent snacks and desserts for your every craving.

BUCKWHEAT GINGER BALLS

• *FRESH OUTTA THE FRIDGE* • *30 MINUTES OR LESS*
• *UNDER 10 INGREDIENTS* • *GLUTEN FREE* • *SOY FREE*
• *NUT FREE* • *OIL FREE* • *NO SUGAR ADDED*

As I've mentioned before, buckwheat is so versatile! You don't even have to cook it and it still works in this super-quick, healthy snack, giving these ginger balls a satisfying crunch.

1 cup (164 g) buckwheat groats
½ cup (73 g) raw sunflower seeds
1 cup (178 g) halved, pitted dates
½ cup (75 g) raisins or currants
1 teaspoon ground ginger
¼ teaspoon salt
2 to 3 tablespoons (30 to 45 ml) water

Pulse buckwheat and sunflower seeds in a food processor equipped with an S-blade until the groats are halved in size. Add the dates, raisins, ginger, and salt to the processor and pulse until the fruit is broken down and the mixture starts clumping together. Add 2 tablespoons (30 ml) water to the "dough" and process until it holds together easily when pinched. Add more water if the mixture is still too dry.

Dampen your hands with water and gently roll 2-tablespoon (25 g)–sized scoops into firm balls. Place the balls in storage container and store at room temperature for 6 to 8 hours or in the refrigerator for up to 14 days.

YIELD: 20 BALLS

NUTRITIONAL ANALYSIS
Per serving (2 balls): 179 calories; 3 g fat; 38 g carbohydrates; 2 g fiber; 19 g sugar; 4 g protein

Tip!
This recipe is super-easy to customize! Try replacing the raisins with dried cherries, apricots, or another type of dried fruit.

YOGURT POPS

• FREEZER FRIENDLY • UNDER 10 INGREDIENTS • GLUTEN FREE
• SOY FREE • NUT FREE • OIL FREE • NO SUGAR ADDED

This snack may seem like a no-brainer, but when warmer weather rolls around, you'll be thanking your previous self for having some of these stocked in your freezer for a cooling, healthy snack!

1½ cups (345 g) vanilla
   nondairy yogurt
½ cup (80 g) diced pineapple
½ cup (75 g) halved
   blueberries

Spoon the yogurt into popsicle molds until the molds are half full. Divide the pineapple and blueberries evenly among the molds and gently press down until the fruit is almost submerged in the yogurt. Fill the molds with the remaining yogurt, then gently tap on the counter to get rid of any air bubbles. Freeze for at least 2 to 3 hours and up to 6 months. (To help get the popsicles out of the molds, run warm water over the molds for 10 to 20 seconds.)

YIELD: 6 (3-OUNCE [85 G]) POPSICLES

NUTRITIONAL ANALYSIS
Per serving: 61 calories; 1 g fat; 13 g carbohydrates; 1 g fiber; 8 g sugar; 1 g protein

CHOCOLATE TAHINI NICE CREAM

• FREEZER FRIENDLY • 30 MINUTES OR LESS • UNDER 10 INGREDIENTS
• GLUTEN FREE • SOY FREE • NUT FREE • OIL FREE • NO SUGAR ADDED

Tip!
If you're a fan of coffee, try adding 1 teaspoon instant coffee granules to the food processor for a mocha vibe.

A lot of the time, after I've finished eating something savory, I crave a little something sweet to close out the meal. This Chocolate Tahini Nice Cream is perfect for this purpose, not only because it's mostly fruit, but also because its flavor is rich enough to soothe that sweet tooth!

4 cups (600 g) chopped
   frozen bananas
½ cup (120 ml) full-fat
   coconut milk
6 tablespoons (90 g) tahini
5 tablespoons (35 g) cocoa
   powder
1 teaspoon vanilla extract
Pinch salt

Puree all ingredients in a food processor equipped with an S-blade until very smooth, scraping down the sides once or twice. (You can make this in a blender, but you may need to add more coconut milk or water.) Store in the freezer for up to 3 months.

YIELD: 6 SERVINGS

NUTRITIONAL ANALYSIS
Per serving: 218 calories; 12 g fat; 26 g carbohydrates; 5 g fiber; 12 g sugar; 5 g protein

CINNAMON TOAST POPCORN

• 30 MINUTES OR LESS • UNDER 10 INGREDIENTS • GLUTEN FREE
• SOY-FREE OPTION • NUT FREE

Did you ever have the super-nutritious breakfast of toast slathered with butter and sprinkled with cinnamon? If so, this snack is going to bring back some memories—and some very delicious memories, at that!.

Tip!
Switch this recipe up by topping the popcorn with your favorite vegan parmesan, nutritional yeast, or chili powder for a savory treat.

3 tablespoons (45 ml) sunflower oil

¾ teaspoon salt, divided

½ cup (105 g) popcorn kernels

3 tablespoons (27 g) coconut sugar

1 teaspoon ground cinnamon

½ teaspoon ground ginger

⅛ teaspoon ground nutmeg

1½ tablespoons (25 ml) melted vegan butter, soy-free if desired

Heat the sunflower oil and ½ teaspoon of the salt in a large pot over medium-high heat. When a drop of water sizzles in the pot, add three popcorn kernels to the oil and cover. Once they have popped, add the remaining popcorn kernels, cover, and adjust the heat to medium.

When nearly all the kernels are popped, remove the pot from the heat and set aside. Combine the coconut sugar, cinnamon, ginger, nutmeg, and remaining ¼ teaspoon salt in a spice grinder and pulse until it becomes a fine powder. Drizzle the melted vegan butter over the popcorn, tossing until evenly coated. Sprinkle the sugar mixture over the popcorn and toss again to coat. Serve warm or allow to cool before transferring to small bags or jars. Store at room temperature for up to 5 days.

YIELD: 6 SERVINGS

NUTRITIONAL ANALYSIS
Per serving: 166 calories; 10 g fat; 17 g carbohydrates; 3 g fiber; 7 g sugar; 2 g protein

LEMON QUINOA BITES

• FRESH OUTTA THE FRIDGE • FREEZER FRIENDLY
• UNDER 10 INGREDIENTS • GLUTEN FREE • OIL FREE

Typically, quinoa is used as a savory base in recipes like my Chimichurri Chickpea Kale Bowls (page 20), but it's also versatile enough to be used for sweet treats! Instead of going for rich flavors like chocolate, these bites have a light and refreshing lemon flavor.

2 cups (475 ml) water
1 cup (173 g) quinoa, rinsed
1 cup (178 g) dried dates, halved and pitted
1 cup (145 g) raw almonds
¼ cup (60 ml) lemon juice plus 1½ tablespoons (9 g) zest
3 tablespoons (45 ml) agave nectar
Pinch salt
½ cup (40 g) quick-cooking oats

Combine quinoa and water in a large pot, cover, and bring to a boil over medium heat. Reduce the heat to medium-low and simmer until water is absorbed, 15 to 18 minutes. Leave the cooked quinoa uncovered for 3 minutes, then fluff with a spoon or fork and set aside to cool.

Pulse cooled quinoa, dates, and almonds in a food processor equipped with an S-blade until the mixture starts clumping together. Add the lemon juice and zest, agave nectar, and salt and pulse until just incorporated, then transfer the mixture to a large bowl. Fold in the oats and knead until well combined. Chill mixture for 20 minutes, then roll 2-tablespoon (30 g)–sized scoops between dampened palms to form balls. Store in the refrigerator for up to 10 days.

YIELD: ABOUT 28 BALLS

NUTRITIONAL ANALYSIS
Per ball: 63 calories; 3 g fat; 8 g carbohydrates; 1 g fiber; 3 g sugar; 2 g protein

Tip!
The bites are great as is, but for a little extra protein and texture, try rolling them in hemp hearts.

SNACKY SEED CLUSTERS

• UNDER 10 INGREDIENTS • GLUTEN FREE • SOY FREE • NUT FREE

One day, I was grocery shopping even though I was hungry—I know, rookie move. I saw some "natural" snacks hanging off an end cap, and scanned the ingredients to see if they were Jackie friendly. Sure enough, they were! And I discovered that they used potato flakes as a binder. My curiosity was piqued, and I knew I had to try something like this at home. So I present to you: Snacky Seed Clusters!

1 cup (160 g) peeled and diced russet potato

3 tablespoons (45 ml) agave nectar

2 teaspoons (10 ml) olive oil

1 teaspoon vanilla extract

¼ teaspoon salt

1 cup (140 g) raw pumpkin seeds (pepitas)

1 cup (21 g) puffed millet cereal

½ cup (50 g) dried cranberries

Preheat the oven to 350°F (180°C, or gas mark 4) and line a baking sheet with parchment paper. Place the potato in a small pot and cover with water. Bring to a boil and then adjust the heat to medium-low, simmering with vented lid until the potato is very tender, about 10 minutes. Drain and rinse with cold water.

Place the cooked potato in a bowl and mash until very smooth using a potato ricer or masher. Add the agave nectar, oil, vanilla, and salt, and whisk until smooth and evenly combined. Fold in the pumpkin seeds, millet, and dried cranberries. Place 2-tablespoon (25 g)–sized scoops about 1 inch (2.5 cm) apart on the prepared baking sheet, and gently flatten each ball so it is about ½ inch (1 cm) thick.

Bake for 60 minutes, until golden brown, carefully flipping clusters halfway through baking. Let cool on a rack for 30 minutes before storing in the pantry for up to 5 days or in the refrigerator for up to 14 days.

YIELD: 20 CLUSTERS

NUTRITIONAL ANALYSIS
Per serving (1 cluster): 66 calories; 3 g fat; 8 g carbohydrates; 1 g fiber; 4 g sugar; 2 g protein

SPINACH-ONION SOUR CREAM DIP

• FRESH OUTTA THE FRIDGE • 30 MINUTES OR LESS • GLUTEN FREE
• SOY FREE • NUT FREE • NO SUGAR ADDED

It seems as though everyone has the same reaction to seeing a bowl of spinach dip: reach for the nearest chip or carrot stick and go to town. My mom makes an amazing spinach dip, but this totally homemade version is a little lighter and perfect for weekday snacking.

2 cups (170 g) frozen chopped spinach, broken into pieces and thawed
1 batch Sunflower Sour Cream (page 166)
2 tablespoons (16 g) minced water chestnuts
2 teaspoons (3 g) minced dried onion
½ teaspoon onion powder
½ teaspoon garlic powder
½ teaspoon dried parsley
¼ teaspoon black pepper
⅛ to ¼ teaspoon salt
6 large carrots, cut into sticks for dipping

Squeeze the thawed spinach in a kitchen towel to remove as much liquid as possible. Transfer spinach to a bowl and fold in the Sunflower Sour Cream, water chestnuts, dried onion, onion powder, garlic powder, dried parsley, black pepper, and salt. Refrigerate for at least 1 hour or up to 7 days. Serve dip with carrot sticks.

YIELD: 4 SERVINGS

NUTRITIONAL ANALYSIS
Per serving: 276 calories; 18 g fat; 22 g carbohydrates; 6 g fiber; 9 g sugar; 11 g protein

SPICY CRUSTED KELP CHIPS

• 30 MINUTES OR LESS • UNDER 10 INGREDIENTS
• GLUTEN-FREE OPTION • SOY FREE • NUT FREE • NO SUGAR ADDED

I know what you're thinking: "Kelp chips? Really, Jackie?" Let me tell you, these kelp chips are the next level up from toasted seaweed snacks. The rice flour coating gives them an amazing crunch, plus makes them a little more filling.

5 sheets nori
1 cup (158 g) brown rice flour
1 teaspoon onion powder
1 teaspoon ground ginger
½ to ¾ teaspoon salt
1 cup (235 ml) water
1 tablespoon (15 g) sriracha or similar chile sauce
½ cup (25 g) panko or gluten-free panko
Cooking spray

Preheat the oven to 375°F (190°C, or gas mark 5), and line two baking sheets with parchment paper. Lay the nori out on the parchment. In a bowl, stir together the brown rice flour, onion powder, ginger, and salt. Stir in the water and sriracha until evenly combined.

Using a pastry brush, apply a thick layer of the batter to each sheet of nori. Sprinkle with panko and spray lightly with cooking spray. Bake for 12 minutes, then switch and rotate baking sheets and bake for an additional 11 to 13 minutes, or until the crumbs start to brown. Let cool on a rack until the chips reach room temperature, then store as whole sheets or break into smaller chip-sized pieces. Store at room temperature for up to 2 weeks.

YIELD: 5 SERVINGS

NUTRITIONAL ANALYSIS
Per serving: 147 calories; 1 g fat; 32 g carbohydrates; 3 g fiber; 1 g sugar; 4 g protein

PEPPERY SEITAN JERKY

• FREEZER FRIENDLY • SOY FREE • NUT FREE

Jerky was one of my favorite road trip foods in my pre-vegan days, so I knew I wanted to make a meaty, high-protein snack that could replace my beloved jerky. This seitan version is one that I have made time and time again because it is that awesome! Plus, you can easily customize the spices in the rub to suit your preferences.

8 ounces (225 g) Seitan Cutlets (page 168)
1 teaspoon onion powder
1 teaspoon chili powder
1 teaspoon paprika
½ teaspoon black pepper
½ teaspoon dried mustard powder
½ teaspoon sugar
½ teaspoon salt

Preheat oven to 300°F (150°C, or gas mark 2) and line a baking sheet with parchment paper. Slice the seitan into ¼-inch (6 mm) thick pieces at an angle. In a shallow dish, combine the onion powder, chili powder, paprika, black pepper, mustard powder, sugar, and salt. Press the two largest sides of the seitan pieces into the spices until lightly coated, then set the seitan on the prepared baking sheet.

Bake for 60 minutes, or until the seitan has darkened in color and become smaller in size, flipping the pieces halfway through baking. Let cool on a rack for at least 20 minutes before transferring to a storage container. Jerky can be stored at room temperature for up to 7 days, in the refrigerator for up to 14 days, or in the freezer for up to 3 months.

YIELD: 4 SMALL SERVINGS

Note: If you made the whole batch of Seitan Cutlets (page 168), use the other 16 ounces (455 g) in recipes like the Seitan Fusion Tacos (page 115) or the Grilled Chimichurri Seitan Salad (page 101)!

NUTRITIONAL ANALYSIS
Per serving: 115 calories; 3 g fat; 11 g carbohydrates; 2 g fiber; 2 g sugar; 11 g protein

GRAIN-FREE GRANOLA

- *FRESH OUTTA THE FRIDGE* • *30 MINUTES OR LESS*
- *UNDER 10 INGREDIENTS* • *GLUTEN FREE* • *SOY FREE* • *OIL FREE*

If you've never made granola before, I assure you that it is really easy to make. Plus, it is great as a stand alone snack—which you'll find out when you try to pack it up—or on top of yogurt, smoothie bowls, and parfaits. I've even made this one grain-free so that more people can enjoy it!

1 cup (140 g) raw pumpkin seeds (pepitas)

1 cup (178 g) pitted and chopped dates

¾ cup (96 g) chopped almonds

¾ cup (64 g) unsweetened coconut flakes

½ cup (73 g) sunflower seeds

¼ cup (44 g) chia seeds

⅓ cup (80 ml) maple syrup

⅓ cup (86 g) smooth almond butter

2 teaspoons (10 ml) vanilla extract

1 teaspoon ground cinnamon

½ teaspoon salt

Preheat oven to 350°F (180°C, or gas mark 4) and line a baking sheet with parchment paper. In a large bowl, combine the pumpkin seeds, dates, almonds, coconut flakes, sunflower seeds, and chia seeds.

In a separate small bowl, whisk together the maple syrup, almond butter, vanilla, cinnamon, and salt until smooth. If the mixture is too thick to stir, add 1 to 2 tablespoons (15 to 30 ml) water to loosen it. Add the maple syrup mixture to the seed and nut mixture and fold together until evenly combined.

Spread the granola out on the baking sheet, pressing into an even layer. Bake for 8 minutes, take the sheet out of the oven and gently stir the granola, then press it down again; the mixture will be pretty loose. Return to the oven and bake for 8 to 10 more minutes, or until the coconut flakes are golden. Let cool on a rack until it reaches room temperature; as it cools it will harden significantly. Store the granola in the refrigerator or in a cool pantry for up to 14 days.

YIELD: 10 SERVINGS (ABOUT ½ CUP [50 G])

NUTRITIONAL ANALYSIS
Per serving: 337 calories; 21 g fat; 28 g carbohydrates; 7 g fiber; 18 g sugar; 7 g protein

ALMOND CRANBERRY BARK

• FRESH OUTTA THE FRIDGE • FREEZER FRIENDLY
• 30 MINUTES OR LESS • UNDER 10 INGREDIENTS
• GLUTEN FREE • SOY FREE • NO SUGAR ADDED

I originally wanted to make almond-cranberry clusters, but the ratios just weren't working out for the number of mix-ins I wanted to use! Taking those flavors and translating them into a delicious chocolate bark ended up being the best-case scenario, because now we have a sweet treat that's not too rich and is even easier to put together.

2 cups (350 g) dairy-free semisweet chocolate chips

3 tablespoons (42 g) refined coconut oil

1½ cups (218 g) whole raw almonds

1 cup (105 g) dried cranberries

1 cup (50 g) unsweetened coconut flakes

½ teaspoon coarse salt

Line a baking sheet with parchment paper, allowing some parchment to hang over the edges of the sheet. In a large, microwave-safe bowl or double-boiler, combine the chocolate chips and coconut oil. Microwave for 90 to 100 seconds or steam over medium-low heat for 3 to 5 minutes. Once the chips have mostly melted, whisk until completely smooth.

Stir in the almonds, cranberries, and coconut flakes and spread the mixture out into an even layer on the parchment paper. Sprinkle coarse salt over the top and freeze for 15 to 20 minutes, or until hard. Use a serrated knife to press down into the bark and chop it into about 16 pieces. Store in the refrigerator or in a cool pantry for up to 14 days, or in the freezer for up to 6 months.

YIELD: 16 SERVINGS

NUTRITIONAL ANALYSIS
Per serving: 267 calories; 17 g fat; 30 g carbohydrates; 2 g fiber; 20 g sugar; 4 g protein

BROWNIE DIP

- *FRESH OUTTA THE FRIDGE* • *30 MINUTES OR LESS*
- *UNDER 10 INGREDIENTS* • *GLUTEN FREE* • *SOY FREE*
- *NUT FREE* • *OIL FREE*

Need a snack that's made out of ingredients that are most likely already in your pantry? This Brownie Dip has you covered! Though the base is legumes, I wouldn't call this a hummus. Low in fat and perfect for any sweet tooth, this dip goes well with apples and graham crackers.

Note: If you can't find low-sodium black beans, just omit the pinch of salt.

1 (15-ounce [425 g]) can low-sodium black beans, drained and rinsed

½ cup (89 g) pitted dates

3 tablespoons (21 g) cocoa powder

2 tablespoons (30 ml) maple syrup

1 to 2 tablespoons (15 to 30 ml) water

1 teaspoon vanilla extract

Pinch salt

Apple slices or vegan graham crackers for dipping

Process black beans, dates, cocoa powder, maple syrup, 1 tablespoon (15 ml) water, vanilla, and salt in a food processor equipped with an S-blade until very smooth. For a thinner consistency, add 1 tablespoon (15 ml) water; the dip should be fairly thick, somewhere between a spread and a hummus. Serve with apples or store in the refrigerator for up to 7 days.

YIELD: 4 SMALL SERVINGS

NUTRITIONAL ANALYSIS
Per serving (without dippers): 205 calories; 1 g fat; 46 g carbohydrates; 8 g fiber; 21 g sugar; 8 g protein

Tip!
If your dates seem dry instead of soft, soak them in hot water for 10 minutes and then strain before using them in this recipe.

PIZZA KALE CHIPS

• 30 MINUTES OR LESS • UNDER 10 INGREDIENTS • GLUTEN FREE
• SOY FREE • NUT FREE • NO SUGAR ADDED

I feel as though kale chips are one of those snacks that are a hard sell to those who haven't tried them. Yet, as you may know, once you do, there's no turning back. Especially not with a batch of Pizza Kale Chips! Truly, I had a hard time keeping my hands off of them until after taking photos.

¼ cup (65 g) tomato paste

2 tablespoons (30 ml) olive oil

1 tablespoon (15 ml) lemon juice

⅓ cup (27 g) nutritional yeast

½ to ¾ teaspoon salt

1 teaspoon dried oregano

1 teaspoon dried basil

1 teaspoon garlic powder

½ teaspoon crushed red pepper, optional

¾ pound (340 g) curly kale, stems removed, torn into bite-sized pieces

Preheat the oven to 350°F (180°C, or gas mark 4), and line two baking sheets with parchment paper. In a large bowl, whisk the tomato paste, olive oil, and lemon juice until smooth. Add the nutritional yeast, salt, oregano, basil, garlic powder, and crushed red pepper and whisk until combined.

Add the kale to the bowl and, using your hands, massage the marinade into the kale until evenly coated, then spread the kale pieces over the prepared baking sheets in a single layer. The pieces do not need much space between them, as they will shrink when baked.

Bake for about 14 minutes, until the chips start to brown and are no longer damp, switching and rotating sheets halfway through baking. Serve immediately or allow the chips to cool completely before transferring to a storage container with a moisture absorbing packet. Chips can be stored at room temperature for up to 10 days.

YIELD: 5 SERVINGS

NUTRITIONAL ANALYSIS
Per serving: 114 calories; 6 g fat; 10 g carbohydrates; 4 g fiber; 4 g sugar; 7 g protein

CHOCOLATE PEANUT BUTTER RICE BARS

• FRESH OUTTA THE FRIDGE • UNDER 10 INGREDIENTS
• GLUTEN FREE • SOY FREE

If, as a kid, you ever had a home-packed lunch, participated in sports, or went to daycare, chances are you ate some small "granola" bars. They were all right and served their purpose, but now it is time for the way-better adult version. These rice bars are easy to make and great for scaling up if you want to double the recipe, depending on the occasion.

4 cups (140 g) brown rice crisps cereal

1 cup (150 g) dairy-free semi-sweet chocolate chips, divided

½ cup (75 g) chopped roasted peanuts

¼ cup (60 ml) agave nectar

¼ cup (65 g) creamy peanut butter

2 tablespoons (14 g) ground flaxseed

3 tablespoons (42 g) refined coconut oil

1½ teaspoons (8 ml) vanilla extract

½ teaspoon coarse salt

Lightly grease an 8 x 8-inch (20 x 20 cm) baking dish, then line it with parchment paper so that the paper hangs over the edges of the pan on two sides. In a large bowl, combine the brown rice crisps, ½ cup (75 g) of the chocolate chips, and the peanuts.

Heat the agave nectar, peanut butter, flaxseed, coconut oil, and vanilla in a small saucepan over medium-low heat until the mixture starts to liquefy. Whisk until smooth, then remove from the heat and pour over the cereal mixture. Fold everything together until there are no dry pockets and the cereal is evenly coated.

Transfer the mixture to the prepared baking dish, and pack it into an even layer using a spatula. Refrigerate the bars for 30 minutes or until they have firmed up considerably (they may still be a little flexible). Microwave the remaining ½ cup (75 g) chocolate chips in a microwave-safe bowl until melted, 45 to 60 seconds. Stir melted chips until very smooth, and use a fork to drizzle the chocolate over the tops of the bars. Sprinkle with the coarse salt, and refrigerate again for at least 10 minutes.

Carefully pull the bars out of the dish using the parchment sling. Cut the rectangle in half widthwise, then slice each half into five bars. Store in the refrigerator for up to 1 month.

Have fun with the bar mix-ins! For some added sweetness, try switching out half of the mixed-in chocolate chips with dried cranberries or diced dates.

YIELD: 10 BARS

NUTRITIONAL ANALYSIS
Per serving (1 bar): 281 calories; 19 g fat; 30 g carbohydrates; 2 g fiber; 15 g sugar; 5 g protein

APPLES WITH TAHINI CARAMEL

• FRESH OUTTA THE FRIDGE • 30 MINUTES OR LESS
• UNDER 10 INGREDIENTS • GLUTEN FREE • SOY FREE
• NUT FREE • OIL FREE

When my sister and I were in elementary school, my parents would often give us apple slices with a little tub of caramel as a snack. Looking back, this may be why I love sweets so much, but that isn't a bad thing! Here's a lighter version of that delicious treat that will keep you satiated between meals.

1 cup (178 g) halved pitted dates
¾ cup (175 ml) hot water
¼ cup (60 g) tahini
2 tablespoons (30 ml) maple syrup
1 teaspoon vanilla extract
½ to ¾ teaspoon salt
4 apples, preferably pink, cored and sliced
1 teaspoon lemon juice (optional)

Combine the dates and hot water in a blender pitcher and let them soften for 10 minutes. Add the tahini, maple syrup, vanilla, and salt and puree until completely smooth. If your blender is struggling, add more water— 1 tablespoon (15 ml) at a time.

If you are saving the apples for later, toss them with the lemon juice to prevent them from browning. The tahini caramel can be stored in the refrigerator for up to 7 days.

YIELD: 4 SERVINGS

NUTRITIONAL ANALYSIS
Per serving: 266 calories; 8 g fat; 52 g carbohydrates; 8 g fiber; 41 g sugar; 3 g protein

Chapter 9

SAUCES, SPREADS, AND MORE

IT WAS THE SPICE GIRLS WHO ONCE SAID, "SAUCE UP YOUR LIFE!" OH, THEY DIDN'T? WELL THEY SHOULD HAVE!

The easiest way to change up a dish is to add a different sauce or spread to it. These components can allow a meal to hop from continent to continent or from light snack to satiating entree. Not only will you find some delicious dressings, there are also delectable dips and other basics to help you out.

GINGER TERIYAKI SAUCE

• *NEEDS SOME HEAT* • *FREEZER FRIENDLY* • *30 MINUTES OR LESS* • *UNDER 10 INGREDIENTS*
• *GLUTEN FREE* • *NUT FREE* • *OIL FREE*

I have got to be honest with you all, ginger is *not* my thing. In baked goods? Sure! Ginger shots? Only because they might make me feel healthier. Otherwise, I'm typically not a fan. But the fresh ginger in this teriyaki sauce is delightful! It adds a kick to what can sometimes be an overly saccharine condiment.

2¼ cups (530 ml) water, divided

¾ cup (170 g) packed brown sugar

⅔ cup (160 ml) tamari

⅓ cup (80 ml) agave nectar

1 tablespoon (8 g) grated fresh ginger or 1 teaspoon ground ginger

2 teaspoons (6 g) minced garlic or ¾ teaspoon garlic powder

3 tablespoons (24 g) cornstarch

3 tablespoons (24 g) toasted sesame seeds

In a medium pot, bring 1½ cups (360 ml) of the water, the brown sugar, tamari, agave nectar, ginger, and garlic to a boil over medium heat. Adjust the heat to medium-low and simmer, stirring occasionally, until the sugar is dissolved, about 3 minutes.

In a small bowl, whisk together the remaining ¾ cup (175 ml) water and the cornstarch and add the slurry to the pot. Whisk until combined, then stir in the sesame seeds. Simmer until the sauce has thickened, 3 to 5 minutes longer.

Store in the refrigerator for up to 2 weeks or in the freezer for up to 6 months.

YIELD: 4 CUPS (945 ML); 16 SERVINGS

NUTRITIONAL ANALYSIS
Per serving: 76 calories; 1 g fat; 17 g carbohydrates; 0 g fiber; 15 g sugar; 2 g protein

PIZZA SAUCE

• FRESH OUTTA THE FRIDGE • FREEZER FRIENDLY • 30 MINUTES OR LESS
• UNDER 10 INGREDIENTS • GLUTEN FREE • SOY FREE • NUT FREE • OIL FREE

This isn't *just* a pizza sauce: This recipe is the foundation from which other sauces grow and upon which toppings are built! Keeping this pizza sauce in your fridge at all times means you're prepared for a variety of dishes, like the Springtime Sheet Pan Polenta Pizza (page 120) or even the high-protein Penne Bolognese (page 113).

3 tablespoons (48 g) tomato paste
2 cloves garlic, minced
1 (15-ounce [425 g]) can tomato sauce
2 teaspoons (9 g) sugar
½ teaspoon onion powder
½ teaspoon dried oregano
½ teaspoon dried basil
Pinch salt
Pinch black pepper

In a small pot, heat the tomato paste and garlic over medium heat until the mixture begins to brown and sizzle, about 2 minutes. Add the tomato sauce, sugar, onion powder, dried oregano, and dried basil and cook, stirring often, until warmed through, 3 to 5 minutes longer. Season with salt and black pepper to taste. Store in the refrigerator for up to 7 days or in the freezer for up to 6 months.

YIELD: 12 OUNCES (355 ML); 4 SERVINGS

NUTRITIONAL ANALYSIS
Per serving: 60 calories; 0 g fat; 14 g carbohydrates; 2 g fiber; 8 g sugar; 2 g protein

KIMCHI CHEESE SAUCE

• NEEDS SOME HEAT • 30 MINUTES OR LESS • GLUTEN FREE
• UNDER 10 INGREDIENTS • SOY FREE • OIL FREE • NO SUGAR ADDED

Years ago, I dedicated full-on months of blogging to vegan mac and cheese, and one of my creations was a kimchi mac. While I was on the right track with my first try, I think I've really perfected the cheese sauce with this recipe. Tangy, savory, and a little spicy, this sauce makes a great base for my new Kimchi Mac and Cheese (page 96)!

1 cup (137 g) raw cashews

¾ cup (98 g) diced carrot

½ cup (110 g) vegan kimchi with brine

3 tablespoons (15 g) nutritional yeast

2 tablespoons (16 g) arrowroot flour

½ teaspoon onion powder

½ teaspoon salt

Combine cashews and carrots in a large pot and cover with water. Cover and bring to a boil, then adjust the heat to medium-low and simmer for 5 minutes. Drain and transfer to a blender. Add 1 cup (235 ml) water, kimchi, nutritional yeast, arrowroot, onion powder, and salt and puree until smooth.

Let mixture rest in the blender for 5 minutes, then blend again to get it as smooth as possible. Store in the refrigerator for up to 7 days.

YIELD: 3 CUPS (710 ML); 4 SERVINGS

NUTRITIONAL ANALYSIS
Per serving: 200 calories; 12 g fat; 14 g carbohydrates; 2 g fiber; 4 g sugar; 8 g protein

If spicy ain't your thing, try sauerkraut instead of kimchi! You may need to adjust the salt accordingly.

CITRUS VINAIGRETTE

• FRESH OUTTA THE FRIDGE • 30 MINUTES OR LESS
• UNDER 10 INGREDIENTS • GLUTEN FREE • SOY FREE • NUT FREE

Vibrant, flavorful, and made with ingredients that you probably have in your kitchen already, this vinaigrette is a great staple to keep in your refrigerator for any salad occasion.

½ cup (120 ml) orange juice plus 1 tablespoon (6 g) zest

2 tablespoons (30 ml) red wine vinegar

2 tablespoons (30 ml) olive oil

2 teaspoons (8 g) Dijon mustard

1 teaspoon agave nectar

¼ teaspoon dried thyme

¼ teaspoon salt

In a bowl or jar with lid, whisk all ingredients until well combined (a milk frother works great as well). Store in the refrigerator for up to 14 days.

YIELD: ¾ CUP (175 ML); 4 SERVINGS

NUTRITIONAL ANALYSIS
Per serving: 83 calories; 8 g fat; 6 g carbohydrates; 0 g fiber; 4 g sugar; 0 g protein

LENTIL WALNUT SAUSAGE CRUMBLES

• NEEDS SOME HEAT • FREEZER FRIENDLY • GLUTEN FREE
• SOY-FREE OPTION • NO SUGAR ADDED

Having multipurpose "crumbles" in your freezer is a game-changer when it comes to meal prepping! Plus, these Lentil Walnut Sausage Crumbles are not too time consuming, and give you way more bang for your buck than store-bought products.

1¾ cups (425 ml) vegetable broth

¾ cup (144 g) green lentils

1½ tablespoons (20 ml) tamari or coconut aminos, divided

½ teaspoon smoked paprika

¼ teaspoon black pepper

1 cup (100 g) walnut halves

½ cup (50 g) quick-cooking oats

1 tablespoon (15 ml) olive oil

1 tablespoon (16 g) tomato paste

½ teaspoon onion powder

1 teaspoon fennel seeds

Salt

In a small pot, bring the vegetable broth, lentils, ½ tablespoon of the tamari, smoked paprika, and black pepper to a boil over medium heat. Adjust the heat to low, cover, and simmer for 10 minutes. Vent the lid and cook until the lentils are tender but not mushy, 15 to 17 minutes longer. Drain any excess liquid (you can store it in the refrigerator to boost the flavor of plain vegetable broth, if desired).

Pulse the lentils and the remaining tamari with the walnuts, oats, olive oil, tomato paste, onion powder, and fennel seed in a food processor equipped with an S-blade until the mixture has become a crumbly dough. Season with salt to taste.

Heat a large, nonstick sauté pan over medium heat and crumble the lentil mixture into large pieces into the pan. Cook until browned, 5 to 7 minutes (you may need to do this in two batches). Let cool, then transfer to a storage container and store in the refrigerator for up to 10 days or in the freezer for up to 3 months.

YIELD: ABOUT 3 CUPS, OR 14 OUNCES (397 G); 4 SERVINGS

NUTRITIONAL ANALYSIS
Per serving: 321 calories; 22 g fat; 22 g carbohydrates; 7 g fiber; 3 g sugar; 11 g protein

Tip!
Switch up the flavor of the crumbles by taking out the fennel seed and adding chili powder, cumin, smoked paprika, or whatever your heart desires.

Note: If you don't have a nonstick pan, spray the pan with a little cooking oil before browning the crumbles.

CILANTRO JALAPEÑO CASHEW DRESSING

• *FRESH OUTTA THE FRIDGE* • *30 MINUTES OR LESS* • *UNDER 10 INGREDIENTS*
• *GLUTEN FREE* • *SOY FREE* • *OIL FREE* • *NO SUGAR ADDED*

This vibrantly green dressing is packed with flavor but is good on dang near anything. And because it is prepared in a blender, it is very easy to make! Raw cashews create a creamy base that carries that herby cilantro goodness and a hint of fresh jalapeño spice.

¾ cup (103 g) raw cashews
¾ cup (175 ml) water
½ cup (8 g) firmly packed fresh cilantro
3 tablespoons (45 ml) lime juice plus
    1 teaspoon zest
1 fresh jalapeño, stemmed and seeded
1 teaspoon onion powder
¾ teaspoon salt
1/8 teaspoon cayenne pepper

Puree cashews, water, cilantro, lime juice and zest, onion powder, salt, and cayenne in a blender until the mixture is as smooth as possible, then let it rest in the pitcher for 5 minutes. Blend again to further break up the cashews. Season with additional salt to taste. Transfer to a jar with a lid and store in the refrigerator for up to 7 days.

YIELD: ABOUT 12 OUNCES (355 ML); 6 SERVINGS

NUTRITIONAL ANALYSIS
Per serving: 117 calories; 8 g fat; 10 g carbohydrates; 2 g fiber; 4 g sugar; 4 g protein

GOCHUJANG AIOLI

• *FRESH OUTTA THE FRIDGE* • *30 MINUTES OR LESS* • *UNDER 10 INGREDIENTS*
• *GLUTEN FREE* • *NUT FREE* • *OIL FREE* • *NO SUGAR ADDED*

Silken tofu is one of my favorite ingredients to use for sauces. It's nearly flavorless, a lean source of protein, and gets super creamy when blended. It's the perfect base for this spicy Gochujang Aioli! This sauce goes great with my Seitan Fusion Tacos (page 115) and Peanutty Tempeh Banh Mi (page 25).

12 ounces (340 g) firm silken tofu
¼ cup (60 g) gochujang
2 tablespoons (30 ml) unseasoned
    rice vinegar
1 clove garlic
1/8 to ¼ teaspoon salt

Puree all ingredients in a blender until completely smooth. Store in the refrigerator for up to 14 days.

YIELD: 14 OUNCES (397 G), 32 SERVINGS

NUTRITIONAL ANALYSIS
Per serving: 27 calories; 1 g fat; 4 g carbohydrates; 0 g fiber; 2 g sugar; 2 g protein

WHITE BEAN GARLIC SPREAD

- **FRESH OUTTA THE FRIDGE • 30 MINUTES OR LESS**
- **UNDER 10 INGREDIENTS • GLUTEN FREE • SOY FREE**
- **NUT FREE • OIL FREE • NO SUGAR ADDED**

White beans make for a great spread base because they don't have a particularly strong flavor like chickpeas or black beans do. Here we have a protein-rich spread that is a hybrid of a mild garlic spread and a hummus. It's great for adding to meals or eating as a snack.

1 [15-ounce [425 g]) can low-sodium white beans, drained with 2 tablespoons [30 ml] liquid reserved

¼ cup (60 g) tahini

3 tablespoons (15 g) nutritional yeast

2 tablespoons (30 ml) lemon juice

1 to 3 tablespoons (15 to 45 ml) water

3 cloves garlic

¾ teaspoon salt

¼ teaspoon black pepper

Puree the white beans and reserved liquid, tahini, nutritional yeast, lemon juice, 1 tablespoon (15 ml) water, garlic, salt, and black pepper in a blender or food processor equipped with an S-blade until very smooth, adding the additional 1 to 2 tablespoons (15 to 30 ml) water to thin it out as needed.

Season with salt to taste. Store in the refrigerator for up to 7 days.

YIELD: ABOUT 1½ CUPS (370 G); 3 SERVINGS

NUTRITIONAL ANALYSIS
Per serving: 128 calories; 5 g fat; 15 g carbohydrates; 5 g fiber; 1 g sugar; 7 g protein

CHIMICHURRI

• FRESH OUTTA THE FRIDGE • FREEZER FRIENDLY • 30 MINUTES OR LESS
• UNDER 10 INGREDIENTS • GLUTEN FREE • SOY FREE • NUT FREE • NO SUGAR ADDED

If you ever have a surplus of herbs on hand—I know that I've bought my fair share of cilantro bunches when I needed only a tiny bit for a garnish—this amazing sauce is what you need! Chimichurri is an Argentinian condiment that is delicious and even a little in-your-face (looking at you, garlic).

1½ cups (24 g) fresh cilantro leaves

1 cup (20 g) fresh flat-leaf parsley leaves

¼ cup (16 g) fresh oregano leaves

¼ cup (60 ml) olive oil

¼ cup (60 ml) red wine vinegar

2 cloves garlic, peeled

½ teaspoon crushed red pepper

¼ teaspoon salt

Some red wine vinegars have added salt. Make sure to use a salt-free vinegar for this recipe!

Pulse cilantro, parsley, oregano, olive oil, red wine vinegar, garlic, crushed red pepper, and salt in a blender or food processor equipped with an S-blade until the mixture is mostly smooth and the herbs are broken up into small pieces. Store in the refrigerator for up to 7 days or in the freezer for up to 3 months.

YIELD: 5 SERVINGS

NUTRITIONAL ANALYSIS
Per serving: 104 calories; 11 g fat; 1 g carbohydrates; 0 g fiber; 0 g sugar; 0 g protein

Tip!
If the garlic is coming off a little too strong for you, try roasting it first, then letting it cool before making this sauce.

VEGGIE BARBECUE SAUCE

• FRESH OUTTA THE FRIDGE • FREEZER FRIENDLY • 30 MINUTES OR LESS
• GLUTEN FREE • SOY-FREE OPTION • NUT FREE • OIL FREE

Making barbecue sauce out of unconventional ingredients is nothing new. Heck, I've made it with strawberries before! But I wanted to make a sneaky veggie version that could be used to incorporate more nutrition into dishes that may not be up to par. Before you get into it, know that I'm a huge fan of Kansas City–style barbecue sauce, so this one is a bit sweet and thick.

1¼ cups (195 g) chopped carrots

1¼ cups (295 ml) water, divided

3 tablespoons (48 g) tomato paste

2 tablespoons (30 ml) molasses

2 tablespoons (30 ml) white vinegar

2 tablespoons (30 ml) tamari or coconut aminos

1 to 2 tablespoons (15 to 30 ml) maple syrup

2 teaspoons (8 g) yellow mustard

1½ teaspoons (4 g) onion powder

1 teaspoon smoked paprika

½ teaspoon chili powder

¼ teaspoon cayenne pepper

Pinch salt

Combine the carrots and ¾ cup (175 ml) of the water in a small pot. Cover and bring to a boil, then adjust the heat to medium-low, and cook until the carrots are very tender, about 8 minutes. Transfer the carrots and cooking water to a blender, followed by the remaining ½ cup (120 ml) water, tomato paste, molasses, vinegar, tamari, maple syrup, mustard, onion powder, smoked paprika, chili powder, cayenne pepper, and salt. Puree until completely smooth, season with salt to taste, then transfer to a sauce pan and simmer for 5 minutes. Store in the refrigerator for up to 14 days or in the freezer for up to 6 months.

YIELD: ROUGHLY 2 CUPS (475 ML)

NUTRITIONAL ANALYSIS
Per serving (8 servings): 44 calories; 10 g fat; 10 g carbohydrates; 1 g fiber; 8 g sugar; 1 g protein

VEGETABLE SCRAP BROTH

• FRESH OUTTA THE FRIDGE • FREEZER FRIENDLY • UNDER 10 INGREDIENTS
• GLUTEN FREE • SOY FREE • NUT FREE • OIL FREE • NO SUGAR ADDED

I hate to admit it, but it took me way too long to make my own veggie scrap broth! I had a bag of odds and ends in my freezer for a couple of years, thinking I'd work up to it. Well, I finally made it, and it was so easy and awesome. There are many recipes throughout the book that you can collect scraps from, so give it a go without hesitation! You can use it in any recipe that calls for vegetable broth.

9 cups (2130 ml) water
1 pound (455 g) onion scraps
8 ounces (225 g) celery
    scraps
6 ounces (170 g) herb and
    greens
    stems/scraps
4 ounces (115 g) carrot
    scraps
4 ounces (115 g) mushroom
    stems
Peel of 1 lemon
2 teaspoons (12 g) salt

Combine the water, onion scraps, celery scraps, herb stems, carrot scraps, mushroom stems, dried mushrooms (use larger amount for earthier flavor) and lemon peel in an Instant Pot or multicooker. Close the lid and bring to high pressure. Once the pot reaches high pressure, cook for 15 minutes. Turn off the heat, quick-release the pressure, stir in salt, and let cool for 15 minutes.

Line a large, fine-mesh strainer with a nut milk bag and set it over a large bowl. Strain the broth, then use the bag to squeeze the remaining liquid from the vegetables. Discard the scraps. Transfer to small storage containers or bags and store in the refrigerator for up to 2 weeks or in the freezer for up to 6 months.

YIELD: ABOUT 3 QUARTS (2.8 LITERS)

SUNFLOWER SOUR CREAM

• FRESH OUTTA THE FRIDGE • 30 MINUTES OR LESS • UNDER 10 INGREDIENTS
• GLUTEN FREE • SOY FREE • NUT FREE • NO SUGAR ADDED

Sour cream is great for adding creamy coolness to dishes, or even as the center of the action in things like Spinach-Onion Sour Cream Dip (page 146)! For a little twist, I went with a nut-free sunflower seed base for this recipe. Make sure to get the raw sunflower seeds, as the toasted and salted impart a little too much unwanted flavor to this condiment.

1 cup (145 g) raw sunflower seeds
6 ounces (175 ml) water
1 tablespoon (15 ml) lemon juice
1 tablespoon (15 ml) olive oil
2 teaspoons (10 ml) white vinegar
½ teaspoon salt

Place the sunflower seeds in a small pot and cover them with water. Cover and bring to a boil, then adjust the heat to medium-low and simmer for 5 minutes. Strain the water from the seeds and transfer the seeds to a blender. Add the water, lemon juice, olive oil, white vinegar, and salt and puree until completely smooth, scraping down the sides a few times. (If you are using a blender, you may need to add more water, 1 tablespoon [15 ml] at a time.) Store in the refrigerator for up to 10 days.

YIELD: ABOUT 2 CUPS (475 ML); 8 SERVINGS

NUTRITIONAL ANALYSIS
Per serving: 112 calories; 11 g fat; 4 g carbohydrates; 2 g fiber; 1 g sugar; 4 g protein

CASHEW RANCH

• FRESH OUTTA THE FRIDGE • 30 MINUTES OR LESS
• UNDER 10 INGREDIENTS • GLUTEN FREE • SOY FREE
• OIL FREE • NO SUGAR ADDED

When you've already made what many people claim is the "best vegan ranch ever," it's hard to top it with another recipe. So instead of straying too far from the "Irresistible Ranch" recipe from *Vegan Bowl Attack!*, I've simplified it and changed only a few things. If you're a ranch lover, you'll be enamored with this one!

⅞ cup (120 g) raw cashews
1 tablespoon (15 ml) white vinegar
1 tablespoon (15 ml) lemon juice
1 teaspoon onion powder
1 teaspoon garlic powder
1 teaspoon dried parsley
1 teaspoon salt
¼ teaspoon black pepper

Place cashews in a small pot and cover them with water. Bring to a boil, then adjust the heat to medium-low, cover, and simmer until the cashews are softened, about 5 minutes. Drain the cashews and rinse them with cold water. Transfer the cashews to a blender, followed by 1 cup (235 ml) water and the vinegar, lemon juice, onion powder, garlic powder, parsley, salt, and black pepper. Blend until smooth, let sit for 5 minutes, then blend again until very smooth. (Ranch will seem thin at first, but will thicken significantly once chilled.) Store in the refrigerator for up to 10 days.

YIELD: 2 CUPS (475 ML); 16 SERVINGS

NUTRITIONAL ANALYSIS
Per serving: 37 calories; 3 g fat; 2 g carbohydrates; 0 g fiber; 0 g sugar; 1 g protein

SEITAN CUTLETS

• NEEDS SOME HEAT • FREEZER FRIENDLY • 30 MINUTES OR LESS
• SOY FREE • NUT FREE • NO SUGAR ADDED

Making your own seitan is easier than you might think and ultimately worth it for the superior quality. Not only is it more cost-efficient, the texture and flavors are better—and customizable. Give this simmered seitan a try if you're looking for a plant-based protein to star in your meals.

FOR THE SEITAN:

1½ cups (200 g) vital wheat gluten

¼ cup (40 g) tapioca flour

3 tablespoons (15 g) nutritional yeast

1 teaspoon salt

½ teaspoon salt-free poultry seasoning

½ teaspoon smoked paprika

1¼ cups (295 ml) vegetable broth

2 tablespoons (30 ml) olive oil

1 tablespoon (16 g) tomato paste

FOR THE SIMMERING BROTH:

2 cups (475 ml) vegetable broth

¼ cup (30 g) roughly chopped yellow onion

3 cloves garlic, crushed

Tip!
I like to make the seitan ahead of time when I need it because once it's refrigerated it is firmer, making it easier to handle and slice.

To make the seitan: In a large bowl, whisk together the vital wheat gluten, tapioca flour, nutritional yeast, salt, poultry seasoning, and smoked paprika. In a liquid measuring cup, stir together the vegetable broth, olive oil, and tomato paste. Fold the broth mixture into the gluten mixture until there are no dry pockets in the dough. Knead for 2 to 3 minutes, then form the dough into a log shape, about 10 inches (25 cm) in length, and set it aside.

To make the simmering broth: In a large pot, bring the vegetable broth, onion, and garlic to a boil over medium heat. Adjust the heat to low so you have a consistent simmer, not a low boil. Cut the seitan log into 10 equal pieces (each will be about 2 ounces [55 g] in weight) and carefully add them to the simmering broth. Adjust the heat, if needed, so that the water is barely moving the seitan pieces. Partially cover and simmer until nearly doubled in size and firm, about 20 minutes, flipping the seitan halfway through cooking.

Remove the seitan from the broth. Seitan can be stored in the refrigerator for up to 7 days or in the freezer for up to 6 months.

YIELD: ABOUT 24 OUNCES (680 G); 6 SERVINGS

NUTRITIONAL ANALYSIS
Per serving: 213 calories; 5 g fat; 19 g carbohydrates; 1 g fiber; 1 g sugar; 22 g protein

Strain the leftover simmering broth through cheesecloth or a fine sieve and use it for another recipe!

VEGAN EGGY SEASONING

• 30 MINUTES OR LESS • UNDER 10 INGREDIENTS • GLUTEN FREE
• SOY FREE • NUT FREE • OIL FREE • NO SUGAR ADDED

After making a few vegan egg–based recipes for this book and realizing that I was scooping out the same five ingredients to season each one, I knew there was a better way. Enter Vegan Eggy Seasoning! You can put this wonderful powder on almost anything and it will taste perfectly eggy without the eggs.

1 cup (80 g) nutritional yeast
4 teaspoons (10 g) onion powder
2 teaspoons (12 g) *kala namak* (Indian black salt; see note below)
1 teaspoon black pepper
1 teaspoon ground turmeric

Combine all ingredients in a blender or food processor equipped with an S-blade and pulse to a fine powder. Allow the dust to settle, then transfer the mix to a jar or storage container and store in a cool pantry for up to 6 months.

YIELD: ABOUT ¾ CUP (106 G); 16 SERVINGS

NUTRITIONAL ANALYSIS
Per serving: 23 calories; 0 g fat; 3 g carbohydrates; 1 g fiber; 0 g sugar; 3 g protein

Note: Kala namak is a sulfur-rich salt that comes from India and is used to impart an eggy flavor to dishes that are egg-free! Despite its name, Indian black salt has more of a rose color when ground. It can be found in Indian markets, some natural food stores, or online.

ACKNOWLEDGMENTS

I didn't think I'd be writing my third cookbook so soon after finishing my second, but here we are! It truly takes a village when it comes to this type of project, and I am so incredibly grateful to everyone involved.

First, thank you to my team of editors and designers at Fair Winds Press/Quarto Publishing and my wonderful literary agent, Marilyn Allen, for making this possible in the first place, and for all of your hard work.

Next, I'd like to thank my partner Corey; without his support I probably would have had a complete mental breakdown in the middle of working on this cookbook. And to my assistant Michael, of Monson Made This fame, your help means the world, and I am so grateful for your skills!

My recipe testers: Wow, y'all really pulled through in an incredible way and I cannot thank you enough. Your testing and input are invaluable, so a big thanks to Billie Fasulo, Lauren Kaufman, Adeline Ramirez, Don Gaines, Michelle Eriksen, Penny Tayler, Jacqueline Chapman, Netty Lam, Hunter Noffsinger, Robynne Mellor, Patty Mondo, Jenni Mischel, Stacey Rothchild, Jenna Nelson, Shelley Osborne, Brianne Hazekamp, and Ashley AKA Moon.

Thank you to my friends Jen, Sandra, Mikey, Chris, and Caitlin for helping me eat all of this food! And to all of my other friends for understanding that finishing up a cookbook means that I go into hibernation for a few months. We'll make up for time lost!

And as always, thank you to my parents for supporting me since the beginning of this winding journey. Who knew it would turn out with me writing three cookbooks in the span of four years?

ABOUT THE AUTHOR

Jackie Sobon is the creator behind the wildly successful food blog *Vegan Yack Attack*, founded in 2011, which is filled with hundreds of delicious recipes accompanied by gorgeous food photos. Her first book, *Vegan Bowl Attack!*, was published in 2016, and her second book, *Vegan Yack Attack on the Go!*, in 2018, both through Fair Winds Press.

Jackie has photographed cookbooks for the likes of Jason Wrobel, *The Happy Herbivore, What the Health*, and many other plant-based brands. She has also self-published three e-books and contributed to *We Love Quinoa* (Quantum, January 2016). She is also the Sweet Treats columnist for *VegNews* magazine, where she develops amazing vegan dessert recipes for the masses. Her work has been featured on KTLA, *SELF* magazine, *Thrive* magazine, PureWow, Buzzfeed, and more.

When she is not contemplating her next creation or obsessing over vegan mac 'n' cheese, she enjoys traveling, crafting, eating with friends, and spending time in the outdoors.

INDEX